Canada, Democracy and the F-35

Canada, Democracy and the F-35

Alan S. Williams

Defence Management Studies Program
School of Policy Studies, Queen's University
2012

Library and Archives Canada Cataloguing in Publication

Williams, Alan S., 1948-
    Canada, democracy and the F-35 / Alan S. Williams.

(The Claxton papers, 1491-137X ; 16)
Includes bibliographical references.
ISBN 978-1-55339-322-1

    1. Canada—Armed Forces—Procurement. 2. Defense contracts—Government policy—Canada. 3. F-35 (Jet fighter plane)—Purchasing—Canada. 4. F-35 (Jet fighter plane). I. Queen's University (Kingston, Ont.). Defence Management Studies Program II. Title. III. Series: Claxton papers ; 16.

UC265.C3W535 2012   355.6'2120971   C2012-901469-9

Copyright © Defence Management Studies Program,
School of Policy Studies, Queen's University, Kingston, 2012

DEDICATION

To my precious grandchildren, Ari and Liam, who bring joy, laughter and love into my life. May they grow up morally, mentally and physically strong, never failing to tell the truth and always willing to serve their country.

The Claxton Papers

The Queen's University Defence Management Studies Program, established with the support of the Canadian Department of National Defence (DND), is intended to engage the interest and support of scholars, members of the Canadian Forces, public servants, and participants in the defence industry in the examination and teaching of the management of national defence policy and the Canadian Forces. The program has been carefully designed to focus on the development of theories, concepts, and skills required to manage and to make decisions within the Canadian defence establishment.

The Chair of the Defence Management Studies Program is located within the School of Policy Studies at Queen's University and is built on the university's strengths in the fields of public policy and administration, strategic studies, management, and law. Among other aspects, the program offers an integrated package of teaching, research, and conferences, all of which are designed to build expertise in the field and to contribute to wider debates within the defence community. An important part of this initiative is to build strong links to DND, the Canadian Forces, industry, other universities, and non-governmental organizations in Canada and in other countries.

This series of studies, reports, and opinions on defence management in Canada is named for Brooke Claxton, Minister of National Defence from 1946 to 1954. Claxton, the first post-Second World War defence minister, was largely responsible for founding the structure, procedures, and strategies that built Canada's modern armed forces. As defence minister, Claxton unified the separate service ministries into the Department of National Defence; revamped the *National Defence Act*; established the office of Chairman, Chiefs of Staff Committee – the first step toward a single chief of defence staff; established the Defence Research Board; and led defence policy through the great defence rebuilding program of the 1950s, the Korean War, the formation of NATO, and the deployment of forces overseas in peacetime. Claxton was unique in Canadian defence politics: he was active, inventive, competent, and wise. It should be recognized that the authors of the Claxton

Papers do so for scholarship purposes only, receiving no compensation for their work.

The author would like to thank colleagues who have shared information and provided clarity to many of the issues surrounding the F-35. In particular, much appreciation to Bill Sweetman, Peter Goon, Dr. Carlo Kopp, Chris Mills, Eric Palmer, Mark Collins and Steve Fuhr.

The author also wishes to thank Carla Douglas for her thorough and professional job as copy editor, as well as Mark Howes and Valerie Jarus for their continued, accomplished efforts to change the work of "mere scholars" into an attractive, readable publication. We all thank Heather Salsbury, Assistant to the Chair, for her unflagging good spirits and willing support to the Chair of Defence Management Studies.

The Chair in Defence Management Studies at the School of Policy Studies is supported in part by a grant to Queen's University from the Department of National Defence within the Security and Defence Forum program.

Ugurhan Berkok
Adjunct Chair, Defence Management Studies Program
School of Policy Studies at Queen's University
Kingston, Ontario
Canada

Contents

Foreword xi

List of Abbreviations xiii

Chapter 1 Joint Strike Fighter Background 1
    History 1
    Planned Design and Performance 1
    Program Structure 3
    International Participation 3
    Expected Delivery Schedule 5

Chapter 2 Canada Enters the JSF Program 7
    Joining the Program 7
    The 2002 MOU 8
    The 2006 MOU 9
    Industrial Benefits 10

Chapter 3 Program Status 15
    Program Development 15
    Cost of Aircraft 16
    Procurement Schedule 18
    Reaction to Program Delays 20

Chapter 4 Canada's Sole-Source Decision 23
    The Announcement 23
    Manipulating the Procurement Process 24
    Misinforming the Public 28

Chapter 5 Closing Observations 41

Notes 43

Annexes..47

Annexes – Source Information 101

About the Author..105

Foreword

On 16 July 2010, the Canadian government announced that it would be acquiring the Lockheed Martin F-35 jet aircraft to replace Canada's aging fleet of CF-18s. Since then, the government has attempted to defend its position by articulating a wide range of misleading statements and by reinterpreting history. It has insulted our intelligence and treated Canadians like naïve children willing to be manipulated at their will. We live in a democracy and, as such, this duly elected government has the authority and power to take such a decision. But in a democracy, citizens also have an obligation – to help ensure that governments are held accountable for their words and their actions. As the person who signed the 2002 Memorandum of Understanding (MOU) on 7 February 2002 with the United States, I am intimately aware of the facts and circumstances regarding Canada's early participation in the program. The government has not been honest with Canadians. If we cannot trust the government on this file, how can we trust it on other files? Nevertheless, I recognize this cynicism is harmful and destructive. Canadians need to be able to trust our politicians. I am hopeful that this publication will help further the public debate over the commitment by the government to purchase the F-35 jet aircraft.

List of Abbreviations

ADM (MAT)	Assistant Deputy Minister for Materiel
AIT	Agreement on International Trade
APUC	Average Procurement Unit Cost
ASTOVL	Advanced Short Take-Off and Vertical Landing
CAS	Chief of the Air Force Staff
CDP	Concept Demonstration Phase
CDR	Canadian Defence Review
CV	Carrier Variant
DARPA	Defense Advanced Research Project Agency
DOD	Department of Defense (US)
DND	Department of National Defence
GAO	Government Accountability Office
IC	Industry Canada
IOC	Initial Operational Capability
IRB	Industrial and Regional Benefits
JAST	Joint Advanced Strike Technology
JSF	Joint Strike Fighter
LRIP	Low Rate Initial Production
NDDN	Standing Committee on National Defence
MOA	Memorandum of Agreement
MOU	Memorandum of Understanding
NM	Nautical Miles
PBO	Parliamentary Budget Officer
PSFD	Production, Sustainment, Follow-On Development

PWGSC	Public Works and Government Services Canada
SAR	Selected Acquisition Report
SDD	System Development and Demonstration
SOR	Statement of Requirements
SLEP	Service Life Extension Program
STOVL	Short Take-Off and Vertical Landing
TPC	Technology Partnerships Canada
US	United States
UK	United Kingdom

CHAPTER 1

Joint Strike Fighter Background

HISTORY[1]

What we know today as the Joint Strike Fighter (JSF) program had its origins in the United States in the 1990s. In late 1993, the US launched its Joint Advanced Strike Technology (JAST) program as a replacement for the US Navy's A6 attack planes and for the US Air Force's replacement of its F-16s.

In 1995, in response to direction by the US Congress, a program led by the Defense Advanced Research Projects Agency (DARPA) to develop an advanced short take-off and vertical landing (ASTOVL) aircraft was incorporated into the JAST program. The name of the program was then changed to Joint Strike Fighter (JSF) to focus on joint development and production of a next-generation jet aircraft.

During the JAST/JSF program's 1994–96 concept development phase, three different aircraft designs were proposed by Boeing, Lockheed Martin, and McDonnell Douglas in a competitive process. On 16 November 1996, the Defense Department announced that Boeing and Lockheed Martin had been chosen to compete in the 1997–2001 Concept Demonstration Phase (CDP).

On 26 October 2001, DOD and the UK selected a team of contractors led by Lockheed Martin to develop and produce the JSF, and dubbed it the Lightning II.

PLANNED DESIGN AND PERFORMANCE[2]

The JSF program envisioned the development and production of three highly common variants: the F-35A, a Conventional Take-Off and Landing (CTOL) variant (and the version Canada has chosen to purchase), the F-35B, a Short Take-Off and Vertical Landing (STOVL) variant, and the F-35C, a Carrier Variant (CV).

FIGURE 1.1
JSF Family of Aircraft

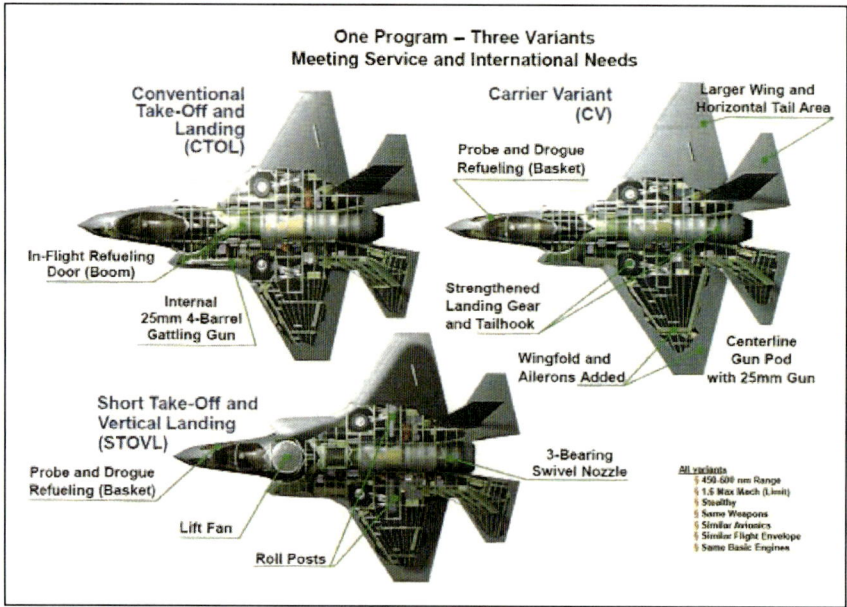

Source: *FrontLine Defence* 1 (2011): 22. www.frontline-canada.com

To control costs, three key principles were established. First, all variants would use a common set of components, systems, and technologies, including engines, avionics, and major structural components of the airframe.

Second, cost containment, referred to as cost-as-an-independent-variable, was established as a fundamental priority for the program. "We said to them, 'This is what we want for capability,'" and then we had a box we wanted to keep them in as far as cost goes," said Kathy Crawford, a spokesperson for the JSF program office.[3] Virtually all contracts would be competed on a best-value basis, and contractors would essentially only be required to meet minimum performance standards and to not exceed maximum allowable costs. Third, recognizing that the more aircraft built the lower the unit cost for each, international participation was welcomed and encouraged with the offer of affordability, timely delivery and leading edge technologies and capabilities. Of particular importance – and this point cannot be overemphasized – was the condition that in order for any country's industries to have an opportunity to compete and win bids in this program, that country had to join the program. As will be discussed below, this was the primary motivator for Canada to become an active partner in the second phase of the program.

The JSF will be powered by the Pratt & Whitney F135 engine. At the direction of the US Congress, the US Department of Defence (DOD) established an alternative engine, the GE F136, to compete with the F135 for JSF production and operations and support contracts. The net cost-benefit of an alternate engine for the JSF program has periodically been debated, and DOD has attempted to eliminate funding for the F136.

The F-35A variant of the JSF will be a single-engine, single-seat aircraft. It is designed to have a range of 1200 nm (2220 km) and to achieve a speed of approximately 1200 miles per hour (1930 km/hour).

It will carry two 2,000 lb weapons internally and AIM-120 AMRAAMs (advanced medium-range air-to-air missiles) with a range of about 26 nm/48 km, depending on altitude.

PROGRAM STRUCTURE

The JSF program was structured in three phases. A concept demonstration phase (CDP) from 1997 to 2002, to prove the concept as being viable and to down-select to a single contractor, with an initial budget of US $5 billion; a system development and demonstration phase (SDD) from 2002 to 2013, to design, develop, test, and build the aircraft in accordance with performance specifications, with a budget of US $41.5 billion; and the production, sustainment and follow-on development phase (PSFD) from 2007 to 2046, to produce and maintain the aircraft, valued at an estimated US $250 billion.

INTERNATIONAL PARTICIPATION[4]

The F-35 program is DOD's largest international cooperative program. As mentioned above, DOD has actively pursued allied participation as a way to defray some of the costs of developing and producing the aircraft. Allies in turn were encouraged to view participation in the F-35 program as an affordable way to acquire a fifth-generation strike fighter, to obtain technical knowledge in areas such as stealth, systems and autonomic logistics, and to allow for industrial opportunities for domestic firms.

Eight allied countries – the UK, Canada, Denmark, the Netherlands, Norway, Italy, Turkey, and Australia – are participating in the F-35 program under an MOU for the SDD and Production, Sustainment, and Follow-On

Development (PSFD) phases of the program. These eight countries have contributed varying amounts of research and development funding to the program, receiving in return various levels of participation in the program. The eight partner countries are expected to purchase hundreds of F-35s, with the UK being the largest anticipated foreign purchaser. It should be noted that as a result of the UK undertaking a defence review, its estimated buy number will likely be known only after 2015. Reports suggest that the UK may cut its order to approximately 50 from 138, while opting out of the STOVL JSF variant in favour of the CV.[5] Two additional countries – Israel and Singapore – are security cooperation participants outside the F-35 cooperative development partnership, and sales to additional countries are possible.

International participation in the F-35 program is divided into three levels according to the amount of money a country contributes to the program – the higher the amount, the greater the nation's voice with respect to aircraft requirements, design, and access to technologies gained during development. Level 1 partner status requires approximately a 10 percent contribution to aircraft development and allows for fully integrated office staff and a national deputy at director level. The UK is the most significant international partner in terms of financial commitment, and the only Level 1 partner. On 20 December 1995, the US and UK governments signed an MOU on British participation in the JSF program as a collaborative partner in the definition of requirements and aircraft design. This MOU committed the British government to contribute US $200 million toward the cost of the 1997–2001 CDP.[6] On 17 January 2001, the US and UK governments signed an MOU finalizing the UK's participation in the SDD phase, with the UK committing to spending US $2 billion, or about 8 percent of the estimated cost of SDD.

Level 2 requires an investment of US $1 billion and was entered into by Italy and the Netherlands, contributing US $1 billion and US $800 million respectively. Australia, Denmark, Norway, Canada, and Turkey joined the F-35 program as Level 3 partners, with contributions ranging from US $125 million to US $175 million.

Analysts say that Britain's – and other allies' – participation in the program makes it much more difficult for the US Congress or administration to cancel the program.[7] In his nomination hearing, DOD acquisition chief Pete Aldridge testified that any decision on the fate of the JSF would have to weigh its "international implications."[8]

EXPECTED DELIVERY SCHEDULE

At the time of the signing of the 2006 PFSD MOU, a total of 3,173 aircraft were to be ordered between 2007 and 2027. Of these, 77 percent, or 2,443, were for the US, and 730 were for the international participants. The peak procurement years would be 2015 through 2021, during which time 160 aircraft would be produced annually (see Annex A of the 2006 MOU, titled Estimated JSF Air Vehicle Procurement Quantities, found in Annex 1 of this book). Deliveries would flow about two years following the order date. Canada's total was for 80 aircraft to be procured at a rate of 10 per year between the years 2014 and 2021 for deliveries in 2016 through 2023. On 10 November 2009, an amendment was made to Annex A in the 2006 MOU. According to the new schedule, Canada was still expected to order 80 aircraft, but the order dates were moved forward. Canada was now scheduled to order 16 aircraft per year between 2014 and 2018 for deliveries between 2016 and 2020.

Subsequently, Canada reduced its intended order to 65 aircraft: 13 to be delivered between 2016 and 2019 and the balance of 52 between 2020 and 2023.[9] What is especially perplexing is the fact that this reduction in quantity from 80 to 65 was announced by Prime Minister Stephen Harper on 12 May 2008,[10] approximately 18 months before the signing of the revised 2006 PFSD MOU. If the reduction was already decided upon, why didn't DND reflect the change in the revised MOU? Were the DND military and civilian officials disputing the reductions with the Prime Minister's Office? Did DND knowingly mislead the US? Furthermore, as the SOR wasn't completed until 2010 (see Chapter 4), how was the number 65 determined? Was it a true reflection of the military's needs or was it a number decided upon by the politicians to fit within the available budget envelope?

CHAPTER 2

Canada Enters the JSF Program

JOINING THE PROGRAM

On 2 January 1998, the Canadian government signed an MOU agreement, committing US $10 million to the JSF program as an observer of its management innovations. However, Canadian officials stated that "there is no commitment to buy the aircraft, and that Canada does not expect the JSF to replace its F/A-18A/Bs (operated as the CF-118A/B since the early 1980s)."[11]

The next decision facing Canada was whether or not to invest in the next phase, the SDD phase. The decision to do so was not based on the need to find an immediate replacement for the Canadian Air Force's tactical fighter, the CF-18. With major investments in the aircraft's airframe and systems, it was anticipated that the CF-18 would remain operational until the 2017 to 2020 timeframe. Rather, the decision was a strategic one. Given the size of this program, it was clear that while there were no guarantees of industrial benefits if one joined the program, it was guaranteed that no business would flow to Canada's aerospace sector if Canada did not participate. True, there were other benefits that would accrue through participation in the program. In particular:

- The information would be invaluable in evaluating the JSF as a potential replacement for the F-18.
- It would help promote interoperability between US, UK, and Canadian militaries.
- DND would gain insight into leading-edge best practices in areas such as autonomic logistics.
- There would be an opportunity to recoup research and development costs should the decision be made to purchase the aircraft.

Nevertheless, the potential impact on Canada's aerospace industry was the overwhelming driver in the decision to pursue an early entry into the program. Surprisingly, Canadian industry did not show much initial interest in participating in the program. Within Canadian industry there was much skepticism as to whether any opportunities would really be open to them. There was doubt that the large investment in time and money would reap any sizable return. In response to these concerns, DND and Industry Canada (IC) officials aggressively marketed the program to the Aerospace Industries Association of Canada and to many of its members, emphasizing the commitment of the government to the program and the strategic opportunity that should not be squandered. By late 2001, industry was on board.

On 7 February 2002, I signed the 2002 SDD MOU (Annex 2), thereby formally committing Canada to the SDD Phase of the JSF program. Canada's financial contribution to this phase was US $100 million over 10 years from DND's budget and US $50 million from Industry Canada's Technology Partnerships Canada (TPC) Program. These funds would be available as loans to Canadian companies to conduct research and development activities for the program.

The next major milestone occurred on 11 December 2006, when Ward Elcock, Deputy Minister of DND, signed the 2006 PFSD MOU, committing Canada to the third phase of the JSF program, the PSFD phase.

THE 2002 MOU

Clause 2.2 of Section II states that its purpose is "to promote industrial and technological cooperation between the United States and Canada during the JSF SDD Phase."

As previously mentioned, Canada contributed $150 million dollars, $100 million from DND and $50 million from Industry Canada's TPC program. For this contribution Canada received significant financial and non-financial benefits.

With respect to the financial benefits, of particular importance are clauses 4.2 and 4.3 in the MOU. Clause 4.2 exempts Canada from paying any of the research and development costs incurred in the program in the event Canada purchases the aircraft. Clause 4.3 provides Canada with levies from sales of the F-35s to third parties. These benefits apply only to those countries that have signed on to the MOU. Consequently, should Canada decide to purchase these aircraft, it should be done through the MOU process. (Essentially the MOU process results in Canada acquiring the aircraft from the US government rather than from Lockheed Martin).

There are also extensive non-financial benefits to participating in the program. By being part of the program, DND gained access to information on leading-edge technologies and systems, on autonomic logistic processes, and on advances in tooling, composites and machining.

Finally, clauses 5.1.1 and 5.3 address Canada's main objective in joining the program. Namely, providing Canadian industry the opportunity to compete for contracts in this program. Clause 5.1.1 states that Canadian bids will be considered and clause 5.3 guarantees that Canada will have access into contract opportunities. Kudos should be given to the DND project team who took it upon themselves to aggressively and proactively inject themselves into the prime contractors' databases to ensure that no valid opportunity to bid was missed.

THE 2006 MOU

As stated in clause 2.1 of the MOU, the overall objective of this MOU was "the cooperative production, sustainment and follow-on development of the JSF Air System to meet the requirements of the Participants." All participants shared the non-recurring costs, based on each participant's expected percentage of aircraft ordered. For the purposes of this MOU, Canada had estimated that it would acquire 80 aircraft. This represented 2.5 percent of the total number of expected quantities ordered. (See Annex A to the 2006 MOU.) These numbers were not set in stone, and as we know, Canada has subsequently lowered its requirement to 65. Accordingly, Canada's contribution to the program was established at US $551 million (clause 5.1). Obviously, as participants changed the quantities in their procurement orders, the financial contributions of each would also change.

It is noteworthy that the MOU contemplated that each country would procure its aircraft in accordance with its respective laws. Specifically, clause 3.2.1.1.1 reads, in part: "Actual procurement of JSF Air Vehicles by the Participants will be subject to the Participants' national laws and regulations and the outcome of the Participants' national procurement decision-making processes." Further, clause 19.1 states in part: "All activities of the Participants under this MOU will be carried out in accordance with their national laws and regulations." In other words, Canada need not twist or manipulate our procurement process in order to buy the F-35s. Section 19 deals with amendments and withdrawals from the MOU. Its clauses are very charitable. In the event of withdrawal, penalties are not extracted but countries are expected to pay their fare share of costs. Clause 19.7 even allows for the withdrawal of the US from this agreement.

INDUSTRIAL BENEFITS

By any objective measure, Canadian industry's success has been outstanding. As of early 2006, 270 Canadian companies were either actively involved with or had expressed interest in JSF opportunities. Figure 2.1 displays the regional distribution of many of these firms and Figure 2.2 displays major awards and commitments.

These awards do not nearly reflect the full extent of Canadian industry's success to date. Here are some noteworthy statistics:

Participation

(a) 376 competitive opportunities were afforded to Canadian industry
(b) Bids were made on 340, or 90 percent, of the opportunities
(c) 144 contracts were won by 65 Canadian companies, universities, and government facilities, a success rate of 42 percent[12]

Contract Values

(a) US $490 million from 144 contracts for the period 2002–12
(b) US $1.1 billion estimated from the current contracts forward for the period 2013–23
(c) US $4.8 to $6.8 billion is the total potential estimated value of JSF work to Canada

Canada's success has not gone unnoticed. In June 2003, the US Department of Defense published a study entitled *JSF International Participation: A Study of Country Approaches and Financial Impacts on Foreign Suppliers*.[13] The study describes the highly proactive approach that has been so effective in gaining JSF business.

Finally, Table 2.1 presents a comparative analysis of the potential return on investment between Canada and three other JSF participants. It is clear that on both an absolute and a comparative basis, Canadian industry has excelled.

FIGURE 2.1 Canadian Firms Identified to JSF Companies

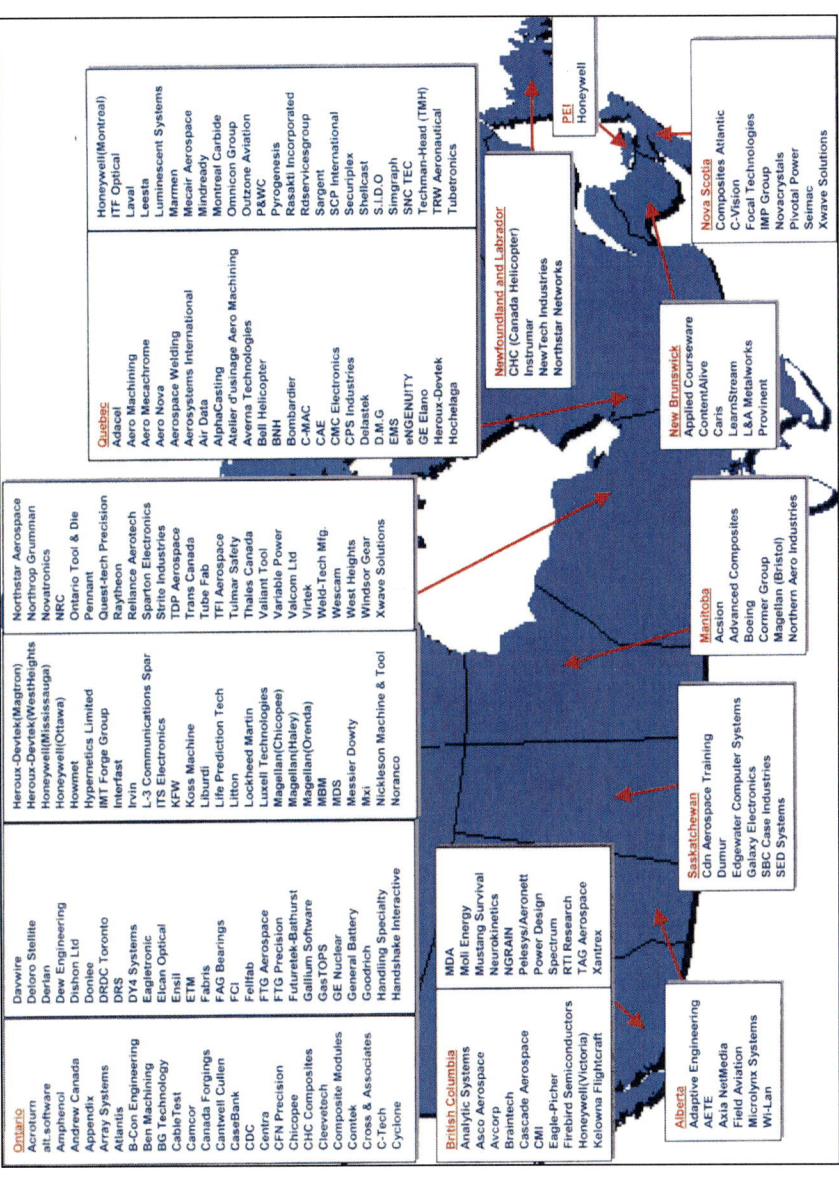

Source: Department of National Defence, *Deck Program Background*, January 2006.

FIGURE 2.2 JSF Design/Production Team Canada, Major Awards and Commitments

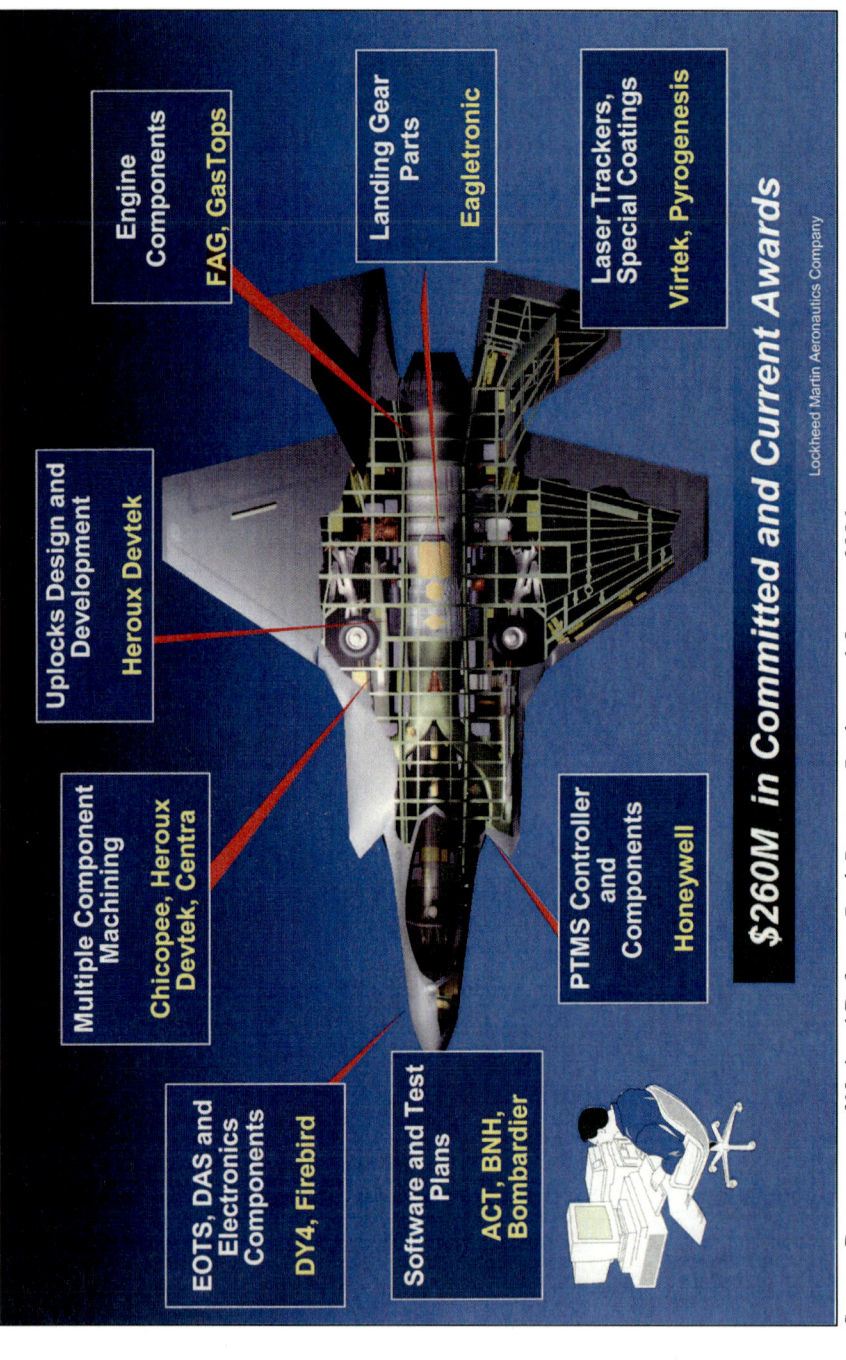

Source: Department of National Defence, *Deck Program Background*, January 2006.

TABLE 2.1
Summary of Partner Country Return Potential

Country	SDD – FRP Revenues 2002–06 (US $Million)	Partnership Investment 2002–06 (US $Million)	Nominal Return 2002–26 (%)	Annually Compounded Rate of Return 2002–26 (%)
United Kingdom	43,456.5	2,056.0	2,113.6	109.2
Italy	4,896.4	1,028.0	476.3	23.8
The Netherlands	5,741.7	800.0	717.7	38.1
Canada	3,910.8	95.0[a]	4,116.6[b]	66.7[c]

Notes

[a] Canada received a $5 million discount from its $100 million commitment due to early payment of participation investment.

[b] Disproportionately high relative to UK due to dramatically lower participation investment.

[c] Canada's annually compounded rate of return is low relative to the UK because of compounding effects from early revenues in the UK program.

Source: Office of the Under Secretary of Defense, *JSF International Participation: A Study of Country Approaches and Financial Impacts on Foreign Supplies* (Washington, DC: GPO, June 2003), p. 4.

CHAPTER 3

Program Status

PROGRAM DEVELOPMENT

The US Government Accountability Office (GAO) serves as the lead auditor of the US government's consolidated financial statements. Most of the agency's work involves program evaluations, policy analyses, and legal opinions and decisions on a broad range of government programs and activities both at home and abroad.[14] In its 15 March 2011 report, the GAO provided a very sombre assessment of the progress achieved in the JSF program. The GAO stated that

> after more than nine years in development and four in production, the JSF program has not fully demonstrated that the aircraft design is stable, manufacturing processes are mature, and the system is reliable. Engineering drawings are still being released to the manufacturing floor and design changes continue at higher rates than desired. More changes are expected as testing accelerates. Test and production aircraft cost more and are taking longer to deliver than expected. Manufacturers are improving operations but have not yet demonstrated a capacity to efficiently produce at higher production rates. Substantial improvements in factory throughput and the global supply chain are needed.

The report continues:

> Development testing is still early in demonstrating that aircraft will work as intended and meet warfighter requirements. Only about four percent of JSF capabilities have been completely verified by flight tests, lab results, or both. Only three of the extensive network of 32 ground test labs and simulation models are fully accredited to ensure the fidelity of results. Software development – essential for achieving about 80 percent of the JSF functionality – is significantly behind schedule as it enters its most challenging phase.[15]

Later in the same report, the GAO continues:

> Over the past year, DOD has substantially restructured the JSF program, taking positive actions that should lead to more achievable and predictable

outcomes. Restructuring has consequences – higher development costs, fewer aircraft in the near term, training delays, and extended times for testing and delivering capabilities to warfighters.

And finally:

Near-term procurement quantities were reduced by 246 aircraft through 2016; the annual rate of increase in production was lowered; and the full-rate production decision moved to 2018, a 5-year slip from the current baseline. The military services were directed to re-examine their initial operational capability (IOC) requirements, the critical need dates when the warfighter must have in place the first increment of operational forces available for combat. We expect the Marine Corps' IOC will slip significantly from its current 2012 date and that the Air Force's and Navy's IOC dates will also slip from the current dates in 2016.[16]

As of November 2011, the development of the JSF has been delayed by at least four years and the development costs have grown by 64 percent from US $34.4 billion in 2001 to US $56.4 billion today.[17]

COST OF AIRCRAFT

Over the past decade, the JSF program has experienced huge cost increases. In March 2010, the US Department of Defense declared that the program experienced a breach of the critical cost growth statutory thresholds (under what is known as the Nunn-McCurdy Act). When a program experiences a Nunn-McCurdy breach of the critical cost growth threshold, DOD is required to take a number of steps, including reassessing the program and submitting a certification to Congress in order to continue the program.[18] (Commonly referred to as Nunn-McCurdy, 10 USC. § 2433 establishes the requirement for DOD to submit unit cost reports on major defense acquisition programs or designated major sub-programs. Two measures are tracked against the current and original baseline estimates for a program: procurement unit cost (total procurement funds divided by the quantity of systems procured) and program acquisition unit cost (total funds for development, procurement, and system-specific military construction divided by the quantity of systems procured). If a program's procurement unit cost or acquisition unit cost increases by at least 25 percent over the current baseline estimate or at least 50 percent over the original baseline estimate, it constitutes a breach of the critical cost growth threshold. Programs are required to notify Congress if a Nunn-McCurdy breach is experienced.)[19]

The Department of Defense subsequently recertified to the US Congress in June 2010 that the JSF program should continue.[20] Table 3.1, below, summarizes the evolution of JSF cost estimates at key junctures in its acquisition history through the 2010 Nunn-McCurdy re-certification. Since then, in January 2011, the Secretary of Defense announced additional development cost increases and further changes consequent to the ongoing restructure, but has not yet established a new approved acquisition program baseline.[21]

TABLE 3.1
Changes in reported JSF Program Cost, Quantities, and Deliveries

	October 2001 (system development start)	December 2003 (2004 replan)	March 2007 (approved baseline)	April 2010 (initial program restructure)	June 2010 (Nunn-McCurdy)
Expected quantities					
Development quantities	14	14	14	15	14
Procurement quantities (US only)	2,853	2,443	2,443	2,443	2,443
Total quantities	2,866	2,457	2,458	2,457	2,457
Cost estimates (then-year dollars in billions)					
Development	$34.4	$44.8	$44.8	$50.2	$51.8
Procurement	196.6	199.8	231.7	277.5	325.1
Military construction	2	0.2	2	0.6	5.6
Total program acquisition	$233.0	$244.8	$278.5	$328.3	$382.5
Unit cost estimates (then-year dollars in millions)					
Program acquisition	$81	$100	$113	$194	$156
Average procurement	69	82	95	114	133
Estimated delivery and production dates					
First operational aircraft delivery	2008	2009	2010	2010	2010
Initial operational capability	2010–2012	2012–2013	2012–2015	2012–2016	TBD
Full-rate production	2012	2013	2013	2016	2016

Note: Does not reflect cost and schedule effects from additional restructuring actions announced after June 2012.
Source: GAO analysis and DOD data.

If you were to ask a salesman for the price of a piece of furniture and the salesman responded that the direct labour cost was $100, how would you react? Most likely, you would be offended and insulted or at the very least, confused. You would know that your final price would be much higher and would include direct material costs, overhead costs and profit. You would feel that the salesman was trying to mislead you. This is precisely what the government has done with respect to the costs of the F-35.

One of the main difficulties with the debate regarding the costs of the F-35 is that there are so many definitions of "cost." For example, there is the "unit recurring flyaway cost," the "total unit flyaway cost," the "procurement unit cost," the "acquisition unit cost" and the "life-cycle cost," to name just a few. Annex 3 describes these costs and shows the relationship between them.

Of all the cost terms, the "unit recurring flyaway cost" is the smallest component of the overall cost. It excludes key costs, such as ancillary equipment, support and training equipment and initial spares. The cost that is a more accurate reflection of the acquisition cost for Canada is entitled the "procurement unit cost," and is commonly referred to as the "average procurement unit cost" or APUC.

As mentioned above, Canada (as well as other signatories to the 2002 MOU) is exempt from paying the research and development, test and evaluation costs associated with the program. This is a huge benefit for Canada and, as such, any costs quoted should exclude these. The APUC does that. It is the APUC, not the unit recurring flyaway cost, that reflects the true cost to Canada to purchase the F-35. Yet it is this unit recurring flyaway cost that the government quotes (at $75 million) as the cost for the F-35A.

As Table 3.1 indicates, the APUC has risen from US $69 million at the launch of the development program in 2001 to US $133 million in 2010, an increase of 92.7 percent. While these figures encompass all three variants, they do reflect the huge cost overruns incurred to date in the program. Chapter 4 will discuss in greater depth the costs Canada can expect to incur in order to acquire and sustain the F-35A.

PROCUREMENT SCHEDULE

Not surprisingly, the developmental delays and the cost escalations in the JSF program have had a significant impact on the procurement schedule of the F-35s. In essence, the US is paying for the increased cost of each aircraft by reducing its annual order. Table 3.2 below reflects the extent to which the orders have "shifted to the right." As noted in Table 3.2, deliveries are expected approximately two years following the order date.

Program Status 19

TABLE 3.2 Air Power Australia Analysis of JSF Program of Record
Historical Record and Independent Assessment of Progressive Decline in Commitments to Buy: USA, Total Program and International Partners

Historical Record and Risk Based Assessments:
Table A-1 Participants' Estimated JSF Air Vehicle Procurement Quantities
(Projected FY of Production Contract Definitization (approximately two years prior to delivery))

Participant	PSFD MoU/ Assessment Date	LRIP 1 CY07	LRIP 2 CY08	LRIP 3 CY09	LRIP 4 CY10	LRIP 5 CY11	LRIP 6 CY12	LRIP 7 CY13	LRIP 8 CY14	LRIP 9 CY15	LRIP 10 CY16	LRIP 11 CY17	LRIP 12 CY18	ChkSum	To CY18 % Feb 07	Delta	ChkSum	To CY17 % Feb 07	Delta
United States	APA Risk Based Assessment: 13 Sep 11								Estimate for end Dec 11: US Proposed minus 100										
CY	13-Sep-11	2	12	14	30	30	32	32	32	81	108	130	130	533	44%	-690	405	38%	-658
CY	11-Nov-10	2	12	14	30	42	45	32	90	113	130	130	130	633	52%	-590	503	47%	-560
CY	Nov-09	2	12	14	30	52	62	71	110	146	130	130	130	809	66%	-414	679	64%	-384
CY	Nov-08	2	12	14	30	43	82	123	110	130	130	130	130	941	77%	-282	811	76%	-252
FY	Feb-07	5	16	47	56	64	103	135	157	160	160	160	160	903	74%	-320	773	73%	-290
Nov 10 as % of Feb 07 Plan		40%	75%	30%	54%	66%	44%	53%	57%	71%	81%	81%	81%	1,223	100%	0	1063	100%	0
TOTALS	APA Risk Based Assessment: 13 Sep 11								Estimate for end Dec 11: US Proposed minus 100										
CY	13-Sep-11	2	12	17	32	30	34	32	41	98	142	180	184	704	40%	-1,070	522	34%	-1,013
CY	11-Nov-10	2	12	17	32	42	51	96	129	179	216	218	213	804	45%	-970	620	40%	-915
CY	Nov-09	2	12	17	32	52	70	156	177	240	227	219	212	1,207	68%	-567	994	65%	-541
CY	Nov-08	2	12	17	32	47	114	126	190	228	229	228	217	1,416	80%	-358	1,204	78%	-331
FY	Feb-07	5	16	50	63	78	142	178	243	252	255	253	239	1,442	81%	-332	1,230	80%	-305
														1,774	100%	0	1535	100%	0
JSF Program Int'l Partner TOTALS	APA Risk Based Assessment: 13 Sep 11													ChkSum	To CY18 % Feb 07	Delta	ChkSum	To CY17 % Feb 07	Delta
APA Assessment																			
CY	13-Sep-11	0	0	3	2	0	2	0	9	17	34	50	54	171	31%	-380	117	25%	-355
CY	11-Nov-10	0	0	3	2	0	6	25	39	66	86	88	83	398	72%	-153	315	67%	-157
CY	Nov-09	0	0	3	2	0	8	33	67	94	97	89	82	475	86%	-76	393	83%	-79
CY	Nov-08	0	0	3	2	4	32	36	80	98	99	98	87	539	98%	-12	457	97%	-15
FY	Feb-07	0	0	3	7	14	39	43	86	92	95	93	79	551	100%	0	472	100%	0

Copyright (c) September 2011, 2007 to 2010: Air Power Australia, PGAA, Peter Goon

For example, in February 2007, a total of 78 jet aircraft were expected to be ordered in 2011. As of September 2011, the expectation is that only 30 jets will be ordered in 2011 (a decrease of 61.5 percent). Table 3.2 also shows the extent to which the cumulative "commitments to buy" out to 2017 and 2018 have declined.

Figure 3.1, below, reflects these same figures in a visual format. It displays the extent to which the planned orders to buy are being reduced and deferred over this period of time.

FIGURE 3.1
Planned Commitments to Buy JSF Aircraft

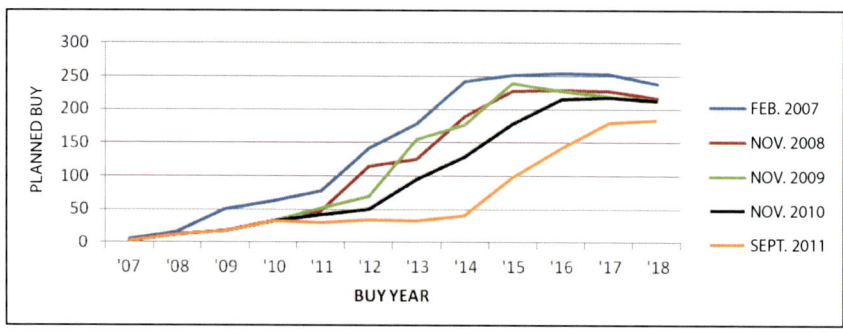

REACTION TO PROGRAM DELAYS

While partner countries in the JSF program react and adapt to the serious problems in the program, Canada remains firm in its pursuit of the F-35. Apparently the huge cost overruns and developmental delays don't faze our leaders. In the House of Commons on 3 November 2011, Minister Fantino said, "The F-35 program is progressing well and on track." Nevertheless, other countries are reacting to the situation and preparing contingency plans. As mentioned above, the UK has deferred its procurement decision until after 2015 and there are reports that they will reduce their order from 138 to 50 aircraft (Annex 4). Australia has launched a review into the F-35 program that "could lead officials to defer the planned order for the first aircraft."[22] Australia is also considering ordering F-18 Super Hornets as a further contingency for the continuing production delays of the F-35s.[23] In the US there is growing pressure to eliminate the program.[24] While this may or may not occur, the US is also cutting back on its orders to pay for the cost overruns. Low Rate Initial Production (LRIP) 5 has been cut further from

35 aircraft to 30 aircraft.[25] The initial plan was for LRIP 5 to produce 78 aircraft. In addition, the US Air Force will be proceeding with a service life extension program (SLEP) and avionics upgrade for 300 to 350 F-16 Fighting Falcons to compensate for an expected delay in the F-35As. This upgrade is expected to cost about US $3 billion.[26] Denmark has yet to confirm its choice of the F-35. It will decide next year, after holding a competition in which the F/A-18E/F Super Hornet is the main challenger.[27]

CHAPTER 4
Canada's Sole-Source Decision

THE ANNOUNCEMENT

On 16 July 2010, the government announced that "it is acquiring the fifth generation Joint Strike Fighter F-35 aircraft to contribute to the modernization of the Canadian Forces, while bringing significant economic benefits and opportunities to regions across Canada" (Annex 5).

The decision to sole-source must have been taken within a few months of the July announcement. Not two months earlier, on 27 May 2010, Peter MacKay, Minister of National Defence, assured his fellow MPs:

27 May 2010, 7:55 p.m.

Peter MacKay

The joint strike fighter program, of which Canada has already made significant investments, will see the next generation fighter capability, will see Canada participate in that program and avail itself of an aircraft that will exceed the current capability. This has been a magnificent aircraft. *This next generation fighter, again, will be an open, competitive, transparent process* (emphasis mine) that will see us receive the best capability, to provide that capability to the best pilots in the world.

27 May 2010, 9:45 p.m.

Peter MacKay

Mr. Chair, the hon. member is mistaken. None whatsoever. I should have referred to this with the more generic term that this is the "next generation" of aircraft. *The joint strike fighter is one of the two aircraft, and there may be others. But I think those are the two main contenders that we are looking at. Obviously we want to get the best value* (emphasis mine), the best aircraft, and we have already embarked upon investments to ensure that happens.

27 May 2010, 9:50 p.m.

Peter MacKay

Mr. Chair, I will come back to that in an instant. *I just want to be very clear on the record that the reference to the next generation of fighter aircraft does not preclude a competition, and an open and transparent one* (emphasis mine). (...) Mr. Chair, I would suggest to the hon. member that regardless of what aircraft we choose, Canadian aerospace has already been a beneficiary of participating in this program.[28]

In March 2010, even Lieutenant-General Andre Deschamps, Chief of the Air Force Staff, anticipated a competitive process. In an interview at that time with *Canadian Defence Review* (published in June 2010), he said the following:

CDR: Where is the next generation fighter on your list of priorities?

CAS: The next generation fighter is very high on my list. We know government wants to get to that discussion soon, and we definitely need to get on with a process to get a new fighter. It sounds like a long time away, but as we know it takes a lot to go through a contracting process and produce a new fighter (Annex 6).

So the unanswered question remains: What happened in the few months before the 16 July 2010 announcement to cause the government to bypass competition and sole-source?

Since the announcement was made, we have learned a great deal about how the procurement process was manipulated and we have observed how the government has continually misrepresented the facts in order to justify its decision. The sections that follow delve into the procurement process and detail the misinformation communicated by the government.

MANIPULATING THE PROCUREMENT PROCESS

In order to understand how the defence procurement process was manipulated to achieve the government's objective, it is first necessary to get a basic understanding of the process. Figure 4.1, below, provides an outline of the competitive defence procurement process.

When spending billions of taxpayers' dollars annually on goods and services for the military, it is essential that the process is open, fair and transparent. For this to occur, the accountabilities of the participants must be clearly defined and adhered to. The process begins with the military

FIGURE 4.1
Defence Procurement Process

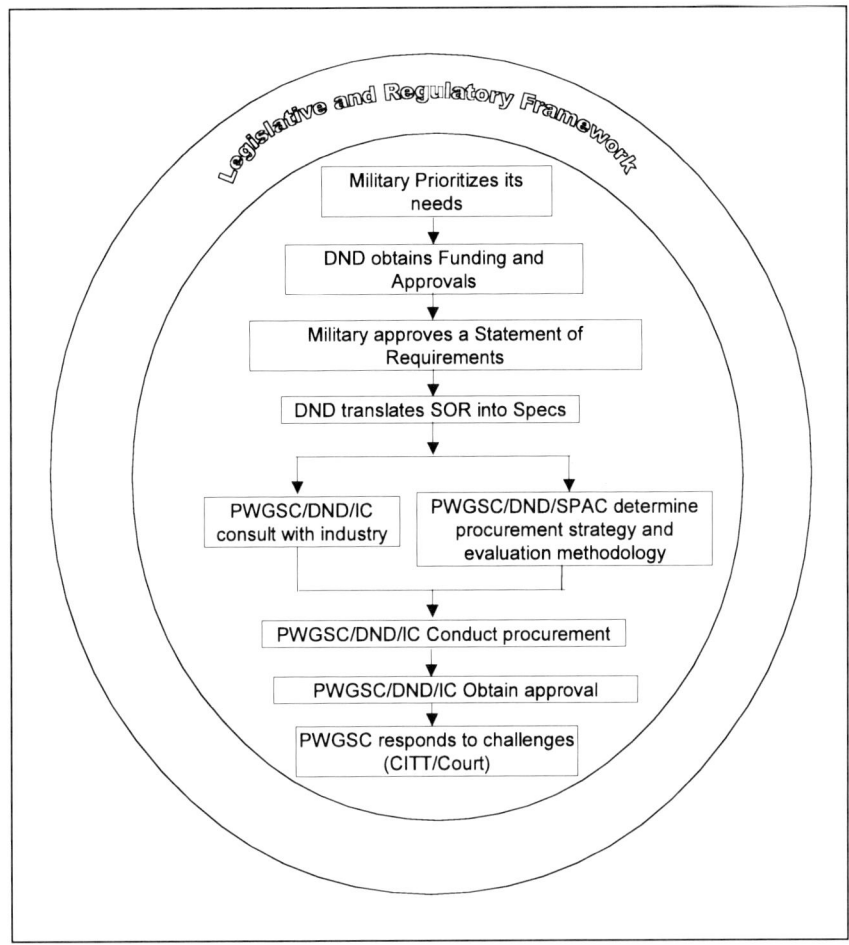

Source: Alan S. Williams, *Reinventing Canadian Defence Procurement: A View from the Inside* (McGill-Queen's University Press, 2006), p. 3.

defining its requirements in a document called the Statement of Requirements, or SOR. Once approved, it is the civillian authorities within DND, Public Works and Government Services Canada (PWGSC) and Industry Canada (IC) who are accountable for conducting the procurement process. Specifically, DND and PWGSC are accountable for translating the SOR into technical specifications, determining the evaluation criteria, specifying the appropriate terms and conditions, releasing the formal request for proposal, evaluating the bids and identifying the successful bidder. IC is responsible for specifying and ensuring that the appropriate kind and level of industrial and regional benefits are obtained. These officials will then obtain the necessary ministerial and/or cabinet approvals to enter into a contract with the winner of the competition.

Sadly, Julian Fantino, Associate Minister for National Defence responsible for defence procurement, is unaware of his accountabilities or of those in his organization. Appearing 25 October 2011 on *Power and Politics*, he was asked a straightforward question from the host of the show, Evan Solomon: "Does the buck stop with you?" In other words, is Minister Fantino accountable for defence procurement? The minister was unable to answer the question with respect to his own accountability. (The reality is that no minister is accountable for defence procurement. In fact, with the appointment of Minister Fantino, the accountability picture has become even more muddied. Now there are three ministers (Ambrose, MacKay and Fantino) whose roles and responsibilities overlap and duplicate. For a more in-depth discussion of this critical issue, please refer to my book, *Reinventing Defence Procurement: A View From The Inside*.) Minister Fantino was also confused regarding the accountabilities of his officials. He emphasized that he takes advice on the F-35 from "the experts who are flying them."[29] That is, from the military. As mentioned above, he is misinformed. He should be taking advice from his civillian leaders, in particular the Deputy Minister and the Assistant Deputy Minister for Materiel (ADM(MAT)) on these matters. They are the ones within DND accountable for defence procurement. The military is accountable for preparing its SOR.

It is also worthwhile noting that since the passage of the Agreement on Internal Trade (AIT) in 1995, the government is precluded from interfering in a competitive procurement process. That is, from the time the government provides approval to proceed with a procurement until it is provided with the results, it is kept in the dark. Three trade agreements have an impact upon federal public sector procurement – the North American Free Trade Agreement, the World Trade Organization – Agreement on Government Procurement, and the Agreement on Internal Trade. However, only the AIT includes defence-specific goods and services and requires competition wherever possible. As a result, any perceived interference in a competitive process could subject the government to legal challenges.

Of course, there are valid reasons to bypass competition and make a sole-source selection. These exceptions are outlined in both the AIT (Annex 7) and in the Treasury Board's contracting guidelines (Annex 8). For example, in the case of an unforeseen emergency, it is acceptable to forego a competition. Rigging an SOR to ensure there is only one qualified bidder, however, is not a valid reason to sole-source.

As mentioned above, the preparation of the SOR is the crucial beginning or foundation for an open, fair and transparent process. Based on this SOR, suppliers are invited to bid and a recommendation is made to the minister on the winning bidder. But in the case of the F-35, the exact opposite sequence of events took place. In 2006, a briefing note by the ADM(MAT) advised the minster that the "JSF family of aircraft has the best operational capabilities to meet Canada's operational requirements, while providing the longest service life and the lowest per aircraft cost of all options considered" (Annex 9). Yet the SOR was only completed in 2010 – four years later!

There are four fundamental issues arising out of the briefing note. First, it precedes the actual SOR by about four years. As such, the procurement process was clearly undermined and manipulated to achieve a predetermined outcome. Can anyone seriously doubt that the SOR was fixed or "wired" to attain the desired result?

Second, the advice in the 2006 briefing note is based on the Air Force's internal analysis. It is not based on the ADM(MAT)'s analysis or conclusions. In effect, the civillian authority, the ADM(MAT), abdicated his accountability by allowing the military to advise on the desired solution.

Third, one wonders how an analysis could have even reached this conclusion given the fact that in 2006 the F-35 was in its very early stages of development. Interestingly, quoted in a December 2006 article in *Inside Defense*, Dave Burt, Canada's Director of Air Requirements, provides a different perspective on the rigour of such an analysis:

> "Up until this point ... a very large part of Canada's program has been about industrial issues and [technology] transfer issues" in the MOU, Burt said. "We have done a relatively modest operational analysis" of this program, he added (Annex 10).

Fourth, as will be made clear in the next section, the military did not have all the necessary information from other suppliers to reach their conclusion that the JSF provided "the longest service life and the lowest per aircraft cost of all options considered."

One final comment on the importance of the SOR. Not only does this document describe the requirements for the jet aircraft but it also addresses a myriad of other critical issues. Properly done, it outlines how the jets assist in fulfilling the government's mandate for the military. It outlines how the jets will support and fit in with the other military assets. It outlines why the specific number of 65 are needed. In short, it provides the answers to basic questions that citizens are entitled to understand before the government spends billions of their tax dollars. To hide this information behind the guise of "national security," as Minister Fantino did,[30] is both wrong and without any basis in fact. SORs are typically unclassified documents available for public dissemination. The information can be conveyed without compromising Canada's national security.

MISINFORMING THE PUBLIC

It was amusing to hear Minister Fantino condemn the "misinformation and misinterpretations" that he and the government had to contend with.[31] It is he and his colleagues who, from the outset, have been misinforming the public and trying to rewrite history regarding the F-35 program. The most frequently heard statements – all false – are the following:

1. There was a competition in 2001, so there is no need to conduct another one.
2. The government was just continuing along the lines established by the previous Liberal government.
3. The F-35 is the best aircraft at the best price.
4. The F-35 will cost US $75 million dollars.
5. Canada needs the F-35 because of the industrial and regional benefits.

I will now address each statement.

1. There was a competition in 2001, so there is no need to conduct another one.

From the outset, the government has endlessly repeated this refrain. In its press release on 16 July 2010, the Honourable Rona Ambrose, Minister of Public Works and Government Services and Minister for Status of Women, said: "A lengthy and intense competition was completed in 2001 for who would build the F-35. Canadian companies and the Canadian government helped develop the F-35, and now we are exercising our option under the Joint Strike Fighter memorandum of understanding to acquire it."[32] Appearing before the Standing Committee of National Defence (NDDN) on 15 September 2010, Tony Clement stated: "We participated in the extensive competitive process to determine who would produce this next-generation fighter and the ultimate selection of Lockheed Martin as the JSF manufacturer in

2001."[33] At the same hearing, Minister Peter Mackay went even further, as is evidenced by this exchange with Jack Harris:

> **Mr. Jack Harris:** Mr. Minister, with respect, I think you're insulting our intelligence to suggest that that competition was about which jet aircraft met Canadian military requirements for the future.
>
> **Hon. Peter MacKay:** That's exactly what it did.
>
> **Mr. Jack Harris:** That was about who would build the jet strike fighter, not about whether or not Canada would purchase it and which one would be –
>
> **Hon. Peter MacKay:** The competition was exactly about what was the right aircraft for Canada.

The government is claiming that the competition conducted in 2001, during which Lockheed Martin was selected over Boeing to build the Joint Strike Fighter, satisfied Canada's requirements. Minister MacKay is wrong and the facts are clear.

First, when the announcement was made on 26 October 2001, only officials from the US and the UK were standing at the podium. As I mentioned earlier, on 20 December 1995 these two countries signed an MOU to establish the UK as a collaborative partner in the definition of requirements and aircraft design. The UK paid dearly for this privilege, contributing US $200 million to the first phase (Canada contributed US $10 million) and US $2 billion to the second phase (Canada contributed US $150 million). The UK, and only the UK, joined the US to be a partner in the 2001 competition that chose Lockheed Martin over Boeing.

Second, for the 2001 competition to have addressed Canada's needs, Canada would have had to determine its requirements and ensured that they were incorporated into the evaluation criteria of the competition. This did not occur. As we now know, Canada's SOR was only finalized in 2010, nine years later, as Lieutenant-General Andre Deschamps indicated when he appeared on *Power and Politics* on 4 November 2010. Further, in its report "Assessing Competitive Strategies for the Joint Strike Fighter: Opportunities and Options" dated March 2001, the Rand authors state: "Canada and Italy participate as Informed Partners. The United States signed an MOU with Canada in January 1998, and an MOA with Italy in December of the same year. Informed Partners do not have the authority to influence requirements."[34]

In the early 2000s, replacing Canada's CF-18s was, pardon the pun, not on our radar. Instead, our focus was on upgrading our existing fleet of CF-18s to ensure they could last until 2017–18. Therefore it should not be surprising that Canada's SOR was not available at the time Lockheed Martin was chosen by the US DOD and the UK Ministry of Defence to build the JSF.

2. The government was just continuing along the lines established by the previous Liberal government.[35]

In making such claims, the government is trying to rewrite history. As the person who signed the 2002 MOU, I can attest that the only reason Canada joined the program was to provide an opportunity for our Canadian industries to participate in the program and be successful in competing for contracts.

Writing in *Ploughshares Monitor* in the summer of 2002, Ken Epps says:

> Alan Williams, the DND Assistant Deputy Minister for Materiel who signed the February Memorandum of Understanding, noted that the JSF agreement was "absolutely essential to support the Canadian aerospace industry. ... Without it, the whole industry would be dramatically eroded" (*Globe and Mail*, 7 February 2002, A16).
>
> Ron Kane, vice-president of the Aerospace Industries Association of Canada, elaborated, linking JSF work to its potential application in the wider commercial aerospace sector: "The JSF is quite critical for Canadian companies to maintain international competitiveness. Other large aerospace projects, including Airbus's A-380 double-decker superjumbo and Boeing's Sonic Cruiser, are expected to employ some of the technologies being developed for the JSF" (ibid.). Furthermore, he added in *Defense News*, "According to Alan Williams, 'the real benefits are not to this department, but it's going to be to industry that participated in all the contracts leading to this and in being a player in this in the future. They're the real winners'" (*Defense News*, 24 July 2000, 42).[36]

Michael Slack, Canada's JSF program manager said in December 2006, "I think that we are going to look at the full spectrum of capabilities to meet future operational requirements. If something emerges that turns out to be extremely capable, who knows? I do not have a crystal ball anymore than you do. Canadian defense officials are eying the 2012 time frame for a final decision on what platform, or mix of platforms, will replace the F/A-18E/F Super Hornets that make up the majority of Canada's fighter fleet." (Annex 10)

It is obvious that there was no intent to sole-source this contract until very recently under the Conservative government. The Liberal government had no such intent.

3. **The F-35 is the best aircraft at the best price.**[37]

This claim has been the government's mantra from the beginning. It has insisted there is no better plane to meet Canada's needs. How does the government know this? Because the military told them so. As such, there is no need to run a competition.

The business of procurement is as much an art as it is a science. If it is guided and shaped by the basic philosophy of competition whenever possible, then such will be the practice. Conversely, if there is a predisposition to sole-source and avoid competition, then ways can always be found to justify this approach and yet appear to comply with the legislation and regulations governing defence procurement. This government has clearly chosen the latter path.

The attempt to sole-source the F-35 is consistent with this government's predisposition to avoid competition.

In 2004, for each dollar contracted over $25,000 for DND, 8.8 cents were contracted non-competitively and 91.2 cents were contracted competitively. In 2009, for every dollar contracted over $25,000 for DND, 42 cents were contracted non-competitively and 58 cents were contracted competitively. This represents nearly a five-fold percentage increase in the value of non-competitive contracts issued between 2004 and 2009. Note also that these figures do not reflect the de facto sole-source contracts like Boeing's C-17 Globemaster strategic lift aircraft, Lockheed Martin's Hercules C-130 tactical lift aircraft and Boeing's CH-47 Chinook medium-to-heavy lift helicopters with a combined contract value of approximately $13 billion dollars.

As the 19 September 2006 briefing note concluded, the military's internal analysis (not made public) established that the F-35 was the best aircraft able to meet the SOR. But can the F-35 really meet all the requirements in the SOR? Also, did the military have all the requisite information to reach that conclusion?

Regarding the capabilities of the F-35, as of the fall of 2011, the F-35 cannot meet the Canadian SOR. The F-35 is many years behind schedule in its development and has no proven operational capabilities. While many people laud its eventual capabilities, there are many skeptics. For example, Air Power Australia conducts in-depth analyses of the JSF Program and the JSF capabilities. It compared the stealth capabilities of the F-35 to those of its main contenders. The F-35 did not fare well (Annex 11).

In a recent air combat simulation exercise, the F-35 was defeated (Annex 12). Adding to these issues is the recognition that the F-35 specifications will be deficient in meeting a number of unique Canadian requirements. These include the requirement for the F-35s to communicate from Canada's north, the requirement for air-to-air refuelling using Probe and Drogue connectors, and the requirement to land on short Arctic runways. It *may* be possible that eventually all of the F-35's problems will be resolved, the Canadian unique modifications will be made, and the jet will live up to its hype. But it also may *not*.

Did the military have all the necessary information to eliminate all other competitors? Not according to Mr. Kory G. Matthews, vice-president, F/A-18E/F Super Hornet program at Boeing. On 4 November 2010, he appeared before the NDDN.[38] In his opening comments, Mr. Matthews stated that the Super Hornet incorporates the latest defence technology advancements, including an integrated display of fused data from a new wide array of sensors, making it the newest combat fighter attack aircraft in operational service today with the United States forces.

He then goes on to reveal that the Canadian Air Force never learned about the high technology of the aircraft. Here is what he told the committee:

> Although some preliminary discussions between Canadian Air Force and United States Navy officials took place in 2008 and early 2009, to our knowledge Canadian officials have not yet received the full complement of Super Hornet performance data from the United States Navy, including those about the aircraft's stealth characteristics.
>
> While security constraints preclude us from having even the most general discussion of this matter in this forum, I can assure you that the Canadian experts will find these briefings most informative and enlightening. I would respectfully suggest that you request this data from the United States Navy, if only to ensure that you make a fully informed decision as part of any next-generation fighter selection process.

Further, in a response to a question from Dominic Leblanc, he reinforced these comments and said "that a full complement of capabilities for this weapons system has not been provided."

Boeing is in a bit of a conundrum because it cannot provide the information directly to DND without a US Government/US Navy release. This release will likely not be forthcoming without a request from the Government of Canada, which would be the norm as part of a competitive process.

I am not suggesting that even with this data, the F-18 Super Hornet could best meet Canada's needs. I am saying that the military's claim to have conducted a rigorous comparison of all alternatives is blatantly false. It is also quite possible that the military did not have all the necessary data from other potential suppliers.

Is the JSF the only jet aircraft capable of replacing our current fleet of CF-18s? With the spiralling costs of the program, the US Congress is at odds over this program. What would Canada do if the program were to be cancelled? Would we say there is no acceptable replacement for our CF-18s? I don't think so. More likely we would redefine our requirements and pick the best available option in the marketplace. Obviously, more than one solution is available to replace our CF-18s, each with its unique advantages and disadvantages. An open, fair and transparent competition sorts these out and determines the best solution for Canada. There is ample time to conduct such a competition. Modifying the statement of requirements to permit an open, fair and transparent competition and undertaking the procurement process can be concluded within two to three years. If we begin in 2012, we can make a decision by 2014. Allowing two years for delivery (the expected lead time in the JSF program), our replacements for our CF-18s would begin to arrive in 2016 or 2017.

With respect to the government's contention that the F-35 can be purchased at the "best price," it is true that if we purchase the F-35 through the MOU (that is, through the US government) it is cheaper than purchasing the F-35 through a contract directly with Lockheed Martin. As explained above, under the MOU, Canada is exempt from paying the research and development costs. However, it is by no means certain that Canada will be acquiring the F-35 at the best price under the MOU. That is to say, it is quite possible that other F-35 partner countries will be able to acquire the aircraft at a lower price than Canada. The reason for this is that the cost any country will pay is dependent upon the number produced during that year. When Canada signed on to the MOU, Canada forecast a requirement for 80 jets to be received during the period 2016 to 2023. These were also to be the peak production years. Since then, Canada has reduced its requirements to 65 aircraft. However, this time frame may no longer represent the peak years of production. With the US looking to reduce its debt load and with production delays and huge cost overruns plaguing the F-35 program, the delivery schedule for the US is being pushed more and more to the right (see Chapter 3).

While no one can be certain about the costs of any jet until a formal bid is received from a potential supplier, it is clear that we can purchase other jet aircraft at a lower cost. For example, see Annex 13 for Boeing cost estimates.

4. The F-35 will cost US $75 million.

As mentioned in Chapter 3, when the government says the cost is US $75 million per aircraft, it is referring to the "recurring flyaway cost." This estimate was reflected in the material the government tabled on 17 March 2010, before the Parliamentary and House Affairs Committee (Annex 14). There are three flaws with this cost estimate. First, it appears to be incomplete. For example, it makes no mention of the incremental cost to refit the aircraft with the satellite communications pod necessary to communicate from the north (Annex 15). Second, this cost estimate is well below that of the US Air Force. In its 2012 budget, presented in February 2011, the US Air Force indicated an expected "unit recurring cost for the F-35A of US $122.9 million," 63.8 percent above that of DND's estimate.[39] Furthermore, the US DOD prepares annual reports on the progress of the JSF. These reports are referred to as Selected Acquisition Reports (SAR). Table 4.1, which follows, is based upon page 29 from the December 2010 SAR report, with the average costs calculated and added to the table.[40]

As is evidenced from the column titled Unit Recurring Flyaway, projecting forward to the year 2030, at no time does the unit recurring flyaway cost drop below US $80 million dollars!

While these two errors are serious, by far the third and most material flaw in the government's US $75 million dollar estimate is that the unit recurring flyaway cost does not reflect the true cost to Canada to acquire the F-35. As mentioned earlier in Chapter 3, the APUC more closely reflects the true cost (i.e., the price) and it is significantly higher.

Table 3.2 shows that from 2001 to June 2010, the average procurement unit cost for all three of the F-35 variants rose from US $69 million to US $133 million. Admittedly, this is an average of all three variants. However, in March 2011, Vice Admiral David Venlet (Annex 16), the new chief of the F-35 Joint Program Office, appeared before a US Congressional committee regarding the F-35s. He told the committee that after his latest review of the program, he is confident in his new cost estimates. For the F-35A (the model Canada plans to acquire), his procurement cost estimate was US $126.6 million (including US $15 million for the engine), just slightly below the US $133 million average.

Second, Israel has purchased 19 F-35As, at an average cost of US $144.7 million. As Israel is only considered a Security Co-operative Participant, their cost includes the research and development, test and evaluation costs of approximately US $23 million for each aircraft. Eliminating this figure from their cost results in an average cost of US $121.7 million.

None of us can know for certain what the final cost to acquire the F-35 will be until we get a firm price quote. As production increases, the costs may drop. On the other hand, in the short to medium term there will be

TABLE 4.1
Extract from 2010 SAR Report

Annual Funding TY$

						F-35A
3010 / Procurement / Aircraft Procurement, Air Force						CTOL

Fiscal Year	Qty	End Item Recurring Flyaway TY $M	Unit Recurring Flyaway TY $M	Non End Item Recurring Flyaway TY $M	Non Recurring Flyaway TY $M	Total Flyaway TY $M
2006	0	117.4	–		–	117.4
2007	2	475.2	237.6		50.1	525.3
2008	6	1,111.4	185.2		207.8	1,319.2
2009	7	1,170.5	167.2		340.2	1,510.7
2010	10	1,475.6	147.6		550.6	2,026.2
2011	22	2,902.6	131.9		675.9	3,578.5
2012	19	2,402.6	126.5		540.4	2,943.0
2013	24	2,690.1	112.1		595.1	3,285.2
2014	40	3,868.6	96.7		482.8	4,351.4
2015	50	4,557.8	91.2		534.8	5,092.6
2016	70	5,639.8	80.6		656.5	6,296.3
2017	80	6,786.8	94.8		906.1	7,692.9
2018	80	6,475.9	80.9		675.6	7,151.5
2019	80	6,474.1	80.9		669.1	7,143.2
2020	80	6,547.3	81.8		666.3	7,213.6
2021	80	6,693.5	83.7		683.5	7,377.0
2022	80	6,883.6	86.0		698.4	7,582.0
2023	80	6,998.3	87.5		710.5	7,708.8
2024	80	7,181.3	89.8		725.0	7,906.3
2025	80	7,310.0	91.4		735.6	8,045.6
2026	80	7,429.9	92.9		751.7	8,181.6
2027	80	7,715.3	96.4		783.9	8,499.2
2028	80	8,032.0	100.4		809.4	8,841.4
2029	80	8,228.5	102.9		822.7	9,051.2
2030	80	8,431.7	105.4		835.9	9,267.6
2031	80	8,639.2	108.0		852.6	9,491.8
2032	80	8,859.5	110.7		871.4	9,730.9
2033	80	9,082.8	113.5		888.7	9,971.5
2034	80	9,241.3	115.5		856.6	10,097.9
2035	73	7,889.5	108.1		550.9	8,440.4
Subtotal	1,763	171,312.1			19,128.1	190,440.2

Source: DOD SAR Report, December 2010, p. 29.

even more upward pressure on the cost of the F-35. The US will likely defer some of its planned order quantities because of the cuts to the Pentagon's budget and because of the many technical problems still plaguing the F-35. International partners like the UK are also facing severe budget pressures and may also reduce their order quantities. Unfortunately for Canada, it still would prefer to procur these jets between 2014 and 2021 in order to replace its current fleet of CF-18s in a timely manner. With all of the deferrals, this period may no longer be the period with maximum production and lowest unit costs.

All evidence to date indicates that we would pay over US $120 million per aircraft, rather than US $75 million, should we decide to acquire this aircraft. At a minimum, the government should be preparing and sharing with Canadians alternative cost and schedule scenarios and back-up plans.

With respect to the life cycle costs, it is important to keep two factors in mind. First, the F-35 is expected to remain operationally effective through the year 2040. Second, while the F-35 is applying leading-edge logistics to help restrain the support costs, these support costs are heavily driven by the complexity of the software. The F-35 is the most software-intensive airplane ever built. The aircraft is estimated to use approximately 5.7 million lines of code, more than double that of the F-22 Raptor. The aircraft and its logistics are expected to use 19 million lines of code![41] Maintaining and upgrading this software are what drive the support costs upward.

In its report on the Joint Strike Fighter dated March 2009, the GAO states: "The total expected investment is now more than US $1 trillion – more than US $300 billion to acquire 2,456 aircraft and US $760 billion in life cycle operation and support costs."[42]

This ratio of the costs to buy versus the costs to support, or about 1 to 2.5, mirrors my experiences at DND. Applying this ratio to Canada's potential purchase would result in a purchase price of $7.8 billion (at $120 million per aircraft), long-term support costs of $19.5 billion, for a total cost of $27.3 billion over approximately 25 years.

An even higher cost projection can be extracted from the latest available SAR on the JSF Program (December 2010). On page 53 of this SAR, a figure of US $1,005.3 billion is reported as the long-term cost to operate and support the aircraft. This results in a costs-to-buy versus costs-to-support ratio of about 3.3, yielding a possible total life cycle cost for Canada over the 25 years of some US $33.5 billion.

Interestingly, on 10 March 2011 the Office of the Parliamentary Budget Officer (PBO) published a report on the life cycle costs of the F-35. Utilizing a distinctly different methodology, the PBO calculated a life cycle cost of US $29.3 billion.[43]

As the above demonstrates, there is still much to learn about how much the F-35A JSF will actually cost, not only to procure but also to operate and support over its projected life cycle of about 25 years.

This begs the question: what if the government maintains its insistence on the F-35, only to discover at the time of signing that the true costs are indeed about double its original estimate? This would necessitate allocating to the F-35 program about an extra US $500 million a year for the next 30 years from DND's capital account, or nearly 25 percent of the funds spent annually on machinery and equipment. As a consequence, many other priority capital acquisitions would be deferred. If I were the chief of the land staff or chief of the maritime staff, I would not be sleeping too well, knowing the impact this would have on my capital priorities.

Finally, what is equally disconcerting is the manner by which the government continues to spin its message regarding costs. For example, on 4 October 2011, Minister Fantino appeared on CBC's *Power and Politics*.[44] When questioned by the host, Evan Solomon, regarding the costs of the F-35, he said, "one figure that I can be absolutely certain about is the US $9 billion dollars for the absolute necessity to acquire these new jets" and "a more honest, ethical response to all of these issues is the US $9 billion dollar figure which will in fact be the ceiling that pertains to what Canada will invest in these particular aircraft." What Minister Fantino labels "more honest" I would call "more obfuscating." Perhaps he expects Canadians to divide US $9 billion by 65 to arrive at a cost per plane of US $138 million each.

The truth is that the government's US $9 billion dollar estimate is essentially comprised of two figures: US $6 billion to buy 65 jets at about US $75 million each, and US $3 billion for other items such as spares, weapons, contingencies and infrastructure. The question then becomes, what if the cost comes in at over US $75 million per plane? Say, at US $120 million. Will the government add an extra US $2.9 billion to its budget? Where will this money come from? Will it be incremental to DND's capital budget? Or will it come from within DND's existing capital budget, thereby necessitating a deferral or a cancellation of other critical military needs? Alternatively, to accommodate the budget shortfall, will the government reduce the number of jets to be purchased? If so, by how many? What would be the operational impact of such a cut?

The military is certainly entitled to know the answers to these questions, as are all Canadians. After all, it is our billions of taxpayers' dollars that are being spent. Minister Fantino said that the government is "being very responsible with taxpayer dollars." Somehow committing to spending billions of our dollars without knowing what these jets will cost, and/or what they will be capable of performing, strikes me as being irresponsible.

5. **Canada needs the F-35 because of the industrial and regional benefits.**

Industrial and regional benefits (IRBs) must never be the main determinant in selecting a winning bid in any defence procurement. The overriding consideration must be the capability of the equipment to meet the requirements of the military. If it cannot, it doesn't matter how good the IRB plan is, the equipment will be rejected. Bidders understand and accept that reality. They also are very much aware of the necessity to submit an IRB plan that meets the criteria established by IC. IRB plans are rated on a pass/fail basis and suppliers work hard to ensure that their bids will get a passing grade. However, listening to government ministers elaborate on the IRB virtues of the F-35, you would wonder what drives the selection – IRBs or meeting the operational requirements of the military?

For example, appearing before the NDDN on 15 September 2010, Tony Clement commented:

> You've hit upon a key point here. Some people ask why sign the contract now. Well, here's the deal. The global supply chain is going to be pretty well put in place by the end of this year. If we did not act now, if we did not move now, we would be running the risk of Canadian companies not being able to bid and compete as part of the global supply chain. Indeed, that's what we were hearing from Canadian industry for the months leading up to the contract. The risk of starting the process all over again is that our companies will not be able to be part of this deal.[45]

This statement makes it clear that Canada committed to buying these jets in July 2010 out of fear that we would lose IRB opportunities, not because it was "the best aircraft at the best price." His testimony strongly suggests that the government now lets Canadian industry determine when and what we buy!

Furthermore, to suggest that if we did not commit now, Canada would lose future opportunities to compete, is absurd. As discussed in Chapter 2, as a signatory to the MOUs, Canada's industry is guaranteed access to business opportunities. A formal commitment to purchase is not necessary. Other partner countries have delayed their commitment. They do not fear being isolated from contract opportunities. Naturally, if I were in charge of a Canadian company that has already won a contract within the JSF program, I too would make this pitch to the government. I would, however, be astonished to find that the government actually bought the argument.

But are the IRBs from the JSF program as great as the government would have us believe? The government is certainly determined to make Canadians think so. In their appearance before the NDDN on 15 September 2011, Ministers MacKay, Ambrose and Clement used the phrase "global supply chain" 30 times![46] I suspect that the backroom communication spin gurus strategized that this term was a winner. However, spinning a yarn over and over doesn't make it true. The fact is that Canada would obtain at least three to four times the IRBs through a competitive process than it would through the MOU framework for the F-35.

Let me explain. As mentioned above, one of the basic principles of the JSF program is to constrain costs by only awarding contracts to those companies that can provide "best value." There are no handouts. Our Canadian companies have performed brilliantly. In Chapter 2, I highlighted the fact that from Canada's initial investment of US $150 million, Canadian companies have won contracts valued at between US $300 million and US $400 million. Government estimates suggest that there are about $12 billion in opportunities. Based on historical success rates, we can be hopeful that Canadian industry will garner US $4 to 6 billion in contracts through the life of the JSF program.

While this amount is large, it pales in comparison to the IRBs that would flow to Canada through a competitive process where all bidders must guarantee IRBs equal to or greater than the value of the contract in order to be declared compliant. In this instance, we will likely have a contract of between US $20–30 billion and guaranteed IRBs of the same amount.

Finally, while contributing to the "global supply chain" has a certain panache to it, the issue of long-term sustainment of the F-35 should be a concern to Canadian industry. Under a competition, bidders would typically ensure that the ongoing support for the equipment takes place in Canada. Under the F-35 MOU, this assurance is nowhere to be seen. Canada maintains a large and highly capable aerospace industry. It would be most unfortunate if our industry lost out on this work.

CHAPTER 5

Closing Observations

As I finalize this manuscript on Remembrance Day, 11 November 2011, I am reminded of the fact that the defence procurement process is not a theoretical, esoteric, bureaucratic process without any real relevance to us. To the contrary, its beneficiaries are the men and women in the military. The lives of these men and women are dependent upon getting the right equipment to the right place at the right time. Putting politics or bureaucracy ahead of their interests is unconscionable.

Yet that is precisely what has occurred with respect to the F-35. The bureaucrats have forsaken their publicly stated commitment for "procuring proven off-the-shelf equipment as opposed to somewhat riskier and lengthier developmental technologies."[47] It's hard to imagine an acquisition more antithetical to this principle than the F-35. The bureaucrats hijacked the procurement process to fulfill their objective of selecting the F-35, not to do what is in the best interests of the military men and women.

Since announcing their intention to acquire the F-35, the government has insulted Canadians' intelligence by repeatedly misinforming and manipulating the facts to suit its agenda. Government officials have tried to rewrite the history of the program. They have refused to release any basic information regarding the acquisition, yet they still feel entitled to spend untold billions of our tax dollars.

To date we have not seen the military's internal analysis, we have not seen the SOR and we have not seen a rigorous analysis of the government's cost estimates. As a result, we do not know whether this acquisition will cost US $16 billion dollars or US $30 billion dollars or more. We do not know whether 65 aircraft is the appropriate number needed to fulfill the role and mandate of the military or whether it is a number merely established to fit within a budget. We do not know exactly what capabilities these jets are supposed to possess and why no other aircraft can fulfill the same functions.

On the other hand, we do know that, as of today, the F-35 does not have the capabilities the government has demanded. We do know that the

JSF program is many years behind in its development. We do know that the costs are continuing to rise at an alarming rate. We do know that the procurement of the F-35s by the US continues to be deferred. And we know that partner countries like the UK, Denmark and Australia are delaying or reviewing their acquisition decisions.

It is irresponsible to commit to buying the F-35 until we can be more certain that it will meet Canada's requirements and until we have firm estimates on the costs to both acquire and provide long-term support for these aircraft.

Only by conducting an open, fair and transparent competition will we know whether the F-35 is or is not the best aircraft for Canada. If it is, it will win the competition.

A major contributor to the chaos in this file is the ministers' and civillian bureaucrats' ignorance of, or total disregard for, their specific roles and accountabilities in the procurement process. As a result, the military has been allowed to not only define its requirements, but also to usurp the civillian authority and make the selection decision.

In one of his *Globe and Mail* Social Studies columns, Michael Kesterton referenced studies conducted at the University of Michigan, which found "that when misinformed people, particularly political partisans, were exposed to corrected facts in news stories, they rarely changed their minds. In fact, they often became even more strongly set in their beliefs. Facts, they found, were not curing misinformation. Like an underpowered antibiotic, facts could actually make misinformation even stronger." No better example of this than the F-35 debacle.

Notes

1. For more information on the history and planned design and performance of the JSF program, please refer to Christopher Bolkcom, Specialist in National Defense: Foreign Affairs, Defense, and Trade Division, CRS Report to Congress, "F-35 Joint Strike Fighter (JSF) Program: Background, Status, and Issues," updated 19 July 2007, pp. CRS2-CRS5.
2. Ibid.
3. Jason Kirby, "Victory in the Skies," *Canadian Business*, 10–23 November 2003, p. 50.
4. For more information on international participation in the JSF program, please refer to Jeremiah Gertler, Specialist in Military Aviation, "CRS F-35 Joint Strike Fighter (JSF) Program: Background and Issues for Congress," 2 April 2010, pp. 10-11.
5. Reuters, "No decision on final UK fighter numbers – officials," 19 October 2010, accessed at http://www.reuters.com/article/2010/10/19/britain-spending-defence-jsf-idUSWEA307220101019; "David Cameron hints aircraft carriers and jet fighters could be axed," *Telegraph*, 4 October 2010, accessed at http://www.telegraph.co.uk/news/uknews/defence/8040404/David-Cameron-hints-aircraft-carrier-and-jet-fighters-could-be-axed.html.
6. "US, UK Sign JAST Agreement," *Aerospace Daily,* 21 December 1995, p. 451.
7. Greg Schneider, "Britain backs Joint Strike Fighter effort," *Washington Post*, 18 January 2001; "British commitment seen as major boost to the Joint Strike Fighter," *Inside the Air Force*, 19 January 2001.
8. Marc Selinger, "JSF decision should weigh 'international implications,' nominee for acquisition post says," *Aerospace Daily,* 27 April 2001.
9. CBC News, "New F-35 jets will miss air force deadline," 15 November 2011, accessed at http://www.cbc.ca/news/politics/story/2011/11/15/f-35-fighter-jets.html.
10. Reuters, "Canada to buy fewer F-35 fighters than thought," 12 May 2008, accessed at http://www.reuters.com/article/2008/05/12/canada-military-idUSN1231405420080512.
11. CRS Report RL 30563 Joint Strike Fighter (JSF) Program: Background, Status and Issues, Updated 8 April 2003, p. 14.

12. DND, *Deck Program Background* (Ottawa: DND, January 2006).
13. A copy of this study is available at www.f-16.net/f-16_forum_download-id-11283.html.
14. For his view on the GAO name and function, see David M. Walker, Comptroller General of the United States, "GAO Answers the Question: What's in a Name?" *Roll Call*, 19 July 2004, accessed at http://www.gao.gov/about/rollcall07192004.pdf.
15. GAO-11-450T, "What GAO Found," 15 March 2011.
16. Ibid., p. 3
17. Gopal Ratnam and Tony Capaccio, "Lockheed's F-35 Costs Rose 64% Over Decade in 'Rich Man's World,'" 3 November 2011, accessed at http://www.bloomberg.com/news/2011-11-03/lockheed-s-f-35-costs-rose-64-over-decade-in-rich-man-s-world-.html.
18. GAO-11-325, p. 4.
19. Ibid.
20. Ibid.
21. GAO-11-325, p. 5.
22. Nigel Pittaway, "Australia launches F-35 review," 27 October 2011, accessed at http://www.defensenews.com/story.php?i=8075152
23. "Australia weighs F-18s if F-35s delayed – Minister," *Dow Jones Deutchland*, 18 October 2011, accessed at http://www.dowjones.de/site/2011/10/australia-weighs-f-18s-if-f35-jets-delayed-minister.html.
24. Matthew Potter, "Senators Levin and McCain send questions on F-35 reprogramming," *Defense Procurement News*, 15 July 2011, accessed at http://www.defenseprocurementnews.com/2011/07/15/senators-levin-and-mccain-send-questions-on-f-35-reprogramming/.
25. Amy Butler, "Pentagon slices F-35 buy to pay for overruns," *Aviation Week*, 31 October 2011, accessed at http://www.aviationweek.com/aw/generic/story.jsp?id=news/asd/2011/10/31/01.xml&headline=Pentagon%20Slices%20F-35%20Buy%20To%20Pay%20For%20Overruns&channel=defense; http://www.f-16.net/f-16_forum_viewtopic-t-16303.html.
26. Bill Carey, "F-35 delay forces $3 billion upgrade request for U.S. Air Force F-16s," *AINOnline*, 4 November 2011, accessed at http://www.ainonline.com/?q=aviation-news/ain-defense-perspective/2011-11-04/f-35-delay-forces-3-billion-upgrade-request-us-air-force-f-16s.
27. Chris Pocock, "Paris 2011: International orders bolster F-35 sales, but so far only five of 597 are firm," AINOnline, 19 June 2011, accessed at http://www.ainonline.com/?q=aviation-news/paris-air-show/2011-06-19/paris-2011-international-orders-bolster-f-35-sales-so-far-only-five-597-are-firm.
28. House of Commons, 27 May 2010, accessed at http://openparliament.ca/hansards/2269/#page=17.

29. CBC News, *Power and Politics* [video clip], 25 October 2011, accessed at http://www.cbc.ca/video/#/News/Politics/Power_&_Politics/1305400780/ID=2160234798.
30. Ibid.
31. Ibid.
32. DND, "Canada's Next Generation Fighter: the F-35 Lightning II," 16 July 2010, accessed at http://www.rcaf-arc.forces.gc.ca/v2/nr-sp/index-eng.asp?id=10749.
33. NDDN, 15 September 2010, accessed at http://www.parl.gc.ca/HousePublications/Publication.aspx?DocId=4653433&Language=E&Mode=1&Parl=40&Ses=3.
34. John Birkler, John C. Graser, et.al., "Assessing Competitive Strategies for the Joint Strike Fighter: Opportunities and Options," National Defense Research Institute, March 2001, accessed at http://www.dtic.mil/cgi-bin/GetTRDoc?AD=ADA390514; p. 13.
35. Jane Taber, "MacKay dodges flak on F-35 jet deficiencies, military belt-tightening," *Globe and Mail*, 24 October 2011, accessed at http://www.theglobeandmail.com/news/politics/ottawa-notebook/mackay-dodges-flak-on-f-35-jet-deficiencies-military-belt-tightening/article2212014/.
36. Ken Epps, "Canada and the Joint Strike Fighter program," *Ploughshares Monitor*, 22 June 2002, accessed at http://www.thefreelibrary.com/Canada+and+the+Joint+Strike+Fighter+program.+(Spotlight+on+Military...-a093792358.
37. DND, "Statement on F35 Variants," accessed at http://www.forces.gc.ca/site/pri/2/pro-pro/ngfc-fs-ft/stovl-eng.asp; DTN News, "Canada F-35 Jets Cost To Soar To $29Billion: Watchdog," 10 March 2011, accessed at http://defensewarnewsupdates.blogspot.com/2011/03/dtn-news-defense-news-canada-f-35-jets.html.
38. NDDN, 4 November 2010, accessed at http://www.parl.gc.ca/HousePublications/Publication.aspx?DocId=4765987&Language=E&Mode=1&Parl=40&Ses=3.
39. US Air Force 2012 Budget, Exhibit P-5, page 3 of 19.
40. DOD, "Selected Acquisition Report (SAR): Joint Strike Fighter," 31 December 2010, accessed at http://www.aviationweek.com/media/pdf/Check6/F-35_SAR_DEC_2010_15_Apr_11.pdf.
41. Graham Warwick, "F-35 JSF – too complicated?" *Aviation Week*, 26 March 2010, accessed at http://www.aviationweek.com/aw/blogs/defense/index.jsp?plckController=Blog&plckScript=blogScript&plckElementId=blogDest&plckBlogPage=BlogViewPost&plckPostId=Blog%3A27ec4a53-dcc8-42d0-bd3a-01329aef79a7Post%3Afe1891f8-92d3-4f98-99ab-77516d2aeafb.
42. GAO Report to Congressional Committees, March 2009, "Joint Strike Fighter Accelerating Procurement before Completing Development Increases the Government's Financial Risk, Highlights," accessed at http://www.gao.gov/htext/d09303.html.

43. Office of the Parliamentary Budget Officer, "An Estimate of the Fiscal Impact of Canada's Proposed Acquisition of the F-35 Lightning II Joint Strike Fighter," 10 March 2011, accessed at http://parl.gc.ca/pbo-dpb/documents/F-35_Cost_Estimate_EN.pdf.
44. "Fantino on F35 costs," CBC News, *Power and Politics* [video clip], 4 October 2011, accessed at http://www.cbc.ca/video/#/News/Politics/Power_&_Politics/1305400780/ID=2148021363.
45. NDDN, 15 September 2010, accessed at http://www.parl.gc.ca/HousePublications/Publication.aspx?DocId=4653433&Language=E&Mode=1&Parl=40&Ses=3.
46. Ibid.
47. NDDN, 1 April 2010, accessed at http://www.parl.gc.ca/HousePublications/Publication.aspx?DocId=4408688&Language=E&Mode=1&Parl=40&Ses=3.

ANNEXES

Annex 1   Extracts from 2006 PSFD MOU

Annex 2   Extracts from 2002 SDD MOU

Annex 3   US Cost Definitions

Annex 4   UK and the JSF

Annex 5   JSF Press Release, 16 July 2010

Annex 6   Interview with Lt.-Gen. Andre Deschamps

Annex 7   AIT

Annex 8   Extracts from Treasury Board Contracting Policy

Annex 9   Briefing Note – September 2006

Annex 10 "UK, Canada Keep JSF Options Open"

Annex 11 APA Stealth Analysis

Annex 12 "F-35 Defeated in Air Combat Simulation"

Annex 13 Boeing's Cost Estimates for the Super Hornet

Annex 14 PBO Cost Estimate for the F-35A

Annex 15 "New Stealth Fighters Lack Ability to Communicate from Canada's North"

Annex 16 "F-35 Production Costs Still Unacceptable, Pentagon Officials Say"

ANNEX 1

Extracts from 2006 PSFD MOU

2.1 The overall objective of the JSF PSFD MOU is the cooperative production, sustainment, and follow-on development of the JSF Air System to meet the requirements of the Participants. This MOU establishes the framework that will enable the Participants to cooperate effectively to accomplish this objective and that will detail their responsibilities and benefits under this MOU.

3.2.1.1.1 The Participants' estimated procurement quantities in Annex A (Estimated JSF Air Vehicle Procurement Quantities) will be used in production planning. Actual procurement of JSF Air Vehicles by the Participants will be subject to the Participants' national laws and regulations and the outcome of the Participants' national procurement decision-making processes. Each Participant's actual procurement quantities of JSF Air Vehicles and propulsion systems will be established in Participant Procurement Requests (PPRs), which will be submitted by that Participant through the procedures described in Section VI (Contracting Provisions).

5.1 The estimate for the total shared costs for the Participants' cooperative efforts under this MOU is 21.876 billion Then Year (TY) U.S. Dollars. Each Participant's maximum contribution to the total shared costs of this MOU is reflected in Table 5-1. In no event will any of these maximum contribution amounts be increased without an amendment to this MOU. However, if a Participant's expenditures reach its maximum contribution amount, the provisions of paragraph 19.5 of Section XIX (Amendment, Withdrawal, Termination, Entry into Effect, and Duration) will apply.

Table 5-1 (In TY U.S. Dollars)

Participant	Maximum Contribution
Australia	$0.690B
Canada	$0.551B
Denmark	$0.33B
Italy	$0.904B
The Netherlands	$0.586B
Norway	$0.33B
Turkey	$0.690B
United Kingdom	$0.952B
United States	$16.843B

19.1 All activities of the Participants under this MOU will be carried out in accordance with their national laws and regulations, including their export control laws and regulations. The responsibilities of the Participants will be subject to the availability of funds for such purposes. If available funds are not adequate to fulfill a Participant's responsibilities, paragraph 5.17 of Section V (Financial Provisions) will apply.

Dec. 11, 2006

ANNEX A

ESTIMATED JSF AIR VEHICLE PROCUREMENT QUANTITIES

The estimated JSF Air Vehicle procurement quantities of the Participants are identified in Table A-1.

Table A-1
Participants' Estimated JSF Air Vehicle Procurement Quantities
(Projected FY of Production Contract Definitization (approximately two years prior to delivery))

Participant	FY07	FY08	FY09	FY10	FY11	FY12	FY13	FY14	FY15	FY16	FY17	FY18
Australia	0	0	0	2	6	14	15	15	15	15	15	3
Canada	0	0	0	0	0	0	0	10	10	10	10	10
Denmark	0	0	0	0	0	0	0	8	8	8	8	8
Italy	0	0	0	0	0	6	6	14	14	14	14	14
Netherlands	0	0	1	2	0	6	10	12	12	12	12	18
Norway	0	0	0	0	0	0	0	8	12	12	12	4
Turkey	0	0	0	0	0	10	10	10	12	12	10	10
United Kingdom	0	0	2	3	8	3	2	9	9	12	12	12
United States	5	16	47	56	64	103	135	157	160	160	160	160
Total	5	16	50	63	78	142	178	243	252	255	253	239

Table A-1
Participants' Estimated JSF Air Vehicle Procurement Quantities (Continued)

Participant	FY19	FY20	FY21	FY22	FY23	FY24	FY25	FY26	FY27	Total	% of Total
Australia	0	0	0	0	0	0	0	0	0	100	3.2%
Canada	10	10	10	0	0	0	0	0	0	80	2.5%
Denmark	8	0	0	0	0	0	0	0	0	48	1.5%
Italy	12	12	12	12	1	0	0	0	0	131	4.1%
Netherlands	0	0	0	0	0	0	0	0	0	85	2.7%
Norway	0	0	0	0	0	0	0	0	0	48	1.5%
Turkey	10	10	6	0	0	0	0	0	0	100	3.2%
United Kingdom	12	12	12	12	12	6	0	0	0	138	4.3%
United States	160	160	160	153	148	118	110	110	101	2443	77.0%
Total	212	204	200	177	161	124	110	110	101	3173	100.0%

ANNEX A

ESTIMATED JSF AIR VEHICLE PROCUREMENT QUANTITIES
AS OF 10 NOV 2009

Table A-1
Participants' Estimated JSF Air Vehicle Procurement Quantities
(Projected FY of Production Contract Definitization (approximately two years prior to delivery))

Participant	CY07	CY08	CY09	CY10	CY11	CY12	CY13	CY14	CY15	CY16	CY17	CY18
Australia	0	0	0	0	0	2	4	8	15	15	15	13
Canada	0	0	0	0	0	0	0	16	16	16	16	16
Denmark	0	0	0	0	0	0	0	8	8	8	8	8
Italy	0	0	0	0	0	4	12	12	12	13	13	13
Netherlands	0	0	1	1	0	2	4	9	10	10	10	10
Norway	0	0	0	0	0	0	0	8	12	12	12	4
Turkey	0	0	0	0	0	0	6	6	12	12	12	12
United Kingdom	0	0	2	1	0	0	7	0	9	11	3	6
United States	2	12	14	30	52	62	123	110	146	130	130	130
TOTALS	2	12	17	32	52	70	156	177	240	227	219	212

Participant	CY19	CY20	CY21	CY22	CY23	CY24	CY25	CY26	CY27	CY28-34	Total
Australia	0	15	13	0	0	0	0	0	0	0	100
Canada	0	0	0	0	0	0	0	0	0	0	80
Denmark	8	0	0	0	0	0	0	0	0	0	48
Italy	12	10	10	10	10	0	0	0	0	0	131
Netherlands	10	10	8	0	0	0	0	0	0	0	85
Norway	0	0	0	0	0	0	0	0	0	0	48
Turkey	12	8	8	8	4	0	0	0	0	0	100
United Kingdom	14	10	2	4	14	14	14	14	13	0	138
United States	130	130	130	130	115	105	103	80	80	509	2443
TOTALS	186	183	171	152	143	119	117	94	93	509	3173

ANNEX 2

Extracts from 2002 SDD MOU

2.2. The Participants intend to promote industrial and technological co-operation between the United States and Canada during the JSF SDD Phase.

4.2. U.S. DoD research and development costs incurred for the Air System will not apply to any Air Systems that may be exported to the CA DND pursuant to U.S. commercial export licenses in accordance with any future cooperative production arrangements. On any future foreign military sale by the U.S. Government to the Canadian Government of the Air System, the U.S. DoD will consider excluding from the price of the Air System all of the U.S. DoD research and development costs incurred for the Air System, provided that the CA DND does not withdraw from the JSF SDD Framework MOU and this Supplement. In any event, the amount of the CA DND research and development costs incurred for the JSF Air System will be excluded from the price of any Air System sold by the U.S. Government to the Canadian Government.

4.3. The Participants recognize that pursuant to paragraph 12.7 of the JSF SDD Framework MOU, they will be given the opportunity to receive levies from sales and other transfers to Third Parties of equipment developed under that MOU in order to recoup their investment in the Project.

5.1.1. Subject to national laws, policies and regulations, the United States will, in evaluating offers from Canadian sources on procurement for defense supplies, at both the prime and subcontract levels, give full consideration, without application of the Buy American Act differentials, to all qualified Canadian offers.

5.3. In order for the CA DND to assure itself that subcontracting competitions are conducted fairly and provide best value, the U.S. DoD will provide the CA DND with insight into the subcontracting for the Project via IPT participation, attendance at Program Management Reviews, and access to the JSF Program Office electronic network.

ANNEX 3

US Cost Definitions

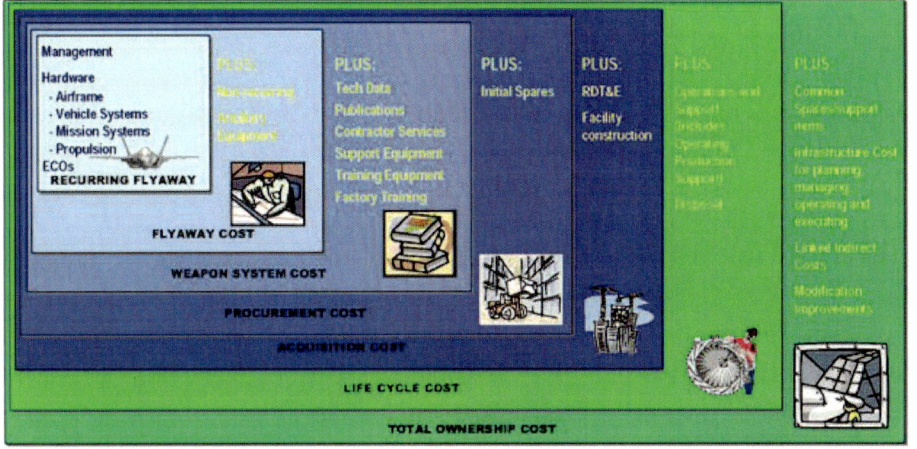

ANNEX 4

UK and the JSF

Canada and the F-35 Procurement: An Assessment

By _____ – October 29, 2010

Author: David S. McDonough

Earlier this year, the Conservative government announced the planned procurement of 65 F-35a Lightening II fighter jets, also called the Joint Strike Fighter (JSF), to replace its aging fleet of CF-18 Hornets. With the first delivery expected in 2016, this aircraft will arrive just as the CF-18s - fresh from a $2.6-billion modernization program to extend their service life - are gradually retired.

This announcement has sparked significant controversy. The government's decision to not seek competitive bids for the CF-18 replacement has raised alarm bells amongst the opposition parties and prominent commentators. And at an estimated cost of $9-billion, and $16-billion if one includes support and maintenance, the sheer price of this equipment purchase has itself proven controversial.

Critics have been particularly vocal on what is essentially the single-sourced nature of the deal, and not without good reason. There were clearly other possible fighter alternatives to the F-35, such as the F/A-18E/F Super Hornet and the Eurofighter Typhoon. The government's claim that only stealthy fifth-generation jet fighters, such as the F-35, were suitable seems a bit disingenuous. Equally, with the venerable CF-18s still having nearly a decade of active service life, Canada does not have any pressing or operational military need for the F-35 platform.

True, the Conservatives have been quick to point out Canada's role as an active participant in and financial contributor to the JSF program. And they warn of the possible economic consequences of not purchasing the fighter, specifically the stunting of Canada's aerospace industry and possible cancellation fees. But Canada's role in the JSF partnership, including its financial contribution to the aircraft's design and development, was a means to secure contracts for its aerospace industry - it did not mean that the country made a definite commitment to purchase the F-35. Alan Williams, recently retired assistant deputy minister for materiel at the Department of National Defence (DND), also points to a withdrawal clause in the 2006 JSF agreement. As he notes, this would allow Canada to drop out of F-35 development with minimal financial costs to pursue an open competition process, and possibly save upwards of $3-billion.

This raises another important concern about the F-35 purchase - namely, the estimated $16-billion price tag. In the current climate of economic uncertainty, this high figure should in itself give one pause.

Importantly, governments tend to underestimate the projected costs of military equipment. One only needs to look at the recent report by the Auditor General Sheila Fraser, which criticizes the ballooning costs and attendant delays in both the Cyclone and sole-sourced Chinook helicopter acquisitions. Similarly, defence contractors recently informed the government that it could not build three Joint Support Ships for the amount that DND had budgeted.

There is a significant risk that the project's cost might increase in the coming years. Officials, however, remain optimistic that such cost increases will not affect Canada's eventual purchase. According to Michael Slack, manager for the F-35 project at DND, Canada will be purchasing the fighter based on the cost of each unit as it is manufactured, thereby avoiding spiraling preproduction costs. Yet one should also avoid being too sanguine on the final cost of the aircraft.

First, it remains to be seen whether the F-35 will also be required to undergo expensive modifications to make it suitable to operate in Canada's unique environment. The sole-sourced Chinooks were similarly modified, and the costs ballooned compared to the off-the-shelf model.

Second, the F-35 purchase price might still significantly increase if the total number of jets manufactured is smaller than expected. Of note, Great Britain has already switched to the cheaper F-35c model and reduced its purchase from 138 to 50, and there is no guarantee that the United States will not follow suit. True, many additional countries might eventually decide to purchase this fighter. But even this cannot be guaranteed.

Third, with little in the way of a maintenance history for the aircraft, there is a possibility that Canada will find the maintenance support costs for the fighter jets to be much higher than the $7-billion projected - this would either result in higher costs or, more likely, a more limited maintenance program. The sole-sourced C-130J Hercules, one should recall, was only afforded seven years of maintenance support rather than the expected 20 years.

That being said, the F-35 might still very well be the most appropriate fighter jet for the Canadian Forces. For one, Canadian companies will likely enjoy some potentially lucrative economic contracts from participating in a major multinational program. Even more importantly, Canada's defence requirements might actually necessitate the acquisition of the F-35. After all, the Conservatives consistently maintain that the F-35, and only a fifth-generation aircraft like the Joint Strike Fighter, is suitable to meet Canada's military needs.

Clearly, the government prefers to discuss the domestic and continental role for these aircraft, due to the uncontroversial nature of such missions and the growing public concern over the future of the Arctic. Indeed, the Conservatives have pointed to Russian bombers testing Canadian air space and used such incidents - routine as they may be - to justify this procurement. And as supporters of the purchase

Annex 4   59

correctly note, friendly relations with Russia and other countries, apart from our immediate and close allies, cannot be guaranteed over the next few decades.

Does this mean that Canada had little choice other than to purchase this expensive fighter jet? Not necessarily. Other fighters, most notably the Super Hornet, represent a significant improvement over our existing CF-18s. Despite lacking some of the more advanced features of the F-35, such as stealth technology, this 4.5-generation aircraft would be more than sufficient to provide surveillance and control over Canadian air space. Importantly, it also represents both a cheaper and more well-tested aircraft than the F-35 - based on how much the US Navy is spending on these aircraft, Canada should expect significant per unit savings, though maintenance costs will likely not be inconsiderate.

True, the Super Hornet would be at a tactical disadvantage when pitted against Russia's forthcoming fifth-generation aircraft, especially the PAK-AF. And the F-35's more sophisticated air-to-air combat and interception capability would prove useful against both Russian fighters and bombers. But this ignores two important points about North American air defence.

First, despite the alarmism that is often generated by Russian nuclear-armed bombers, this threat is only actualized in the event that Russia threatens a significant nuclear attack on North America. And the primary means of dealing with this possibility is not by robust air defence systems, in which the more advanced F-35s would offer definite advantage, but rather by early detection and warning - this helps to ensure a survivable American nuclear arsenal capable of retaliating, and thereby deterring, such aggression.

Second, while Russia might still violate and infringe upon Canadian airspace, one should not overlook the crucial role played by our superpower ally. Russia would be forced to deal not only with the Canadian air force, but also the much more sizable American fleet. Simply put, it would matter little to the Russians whether Canada was armed with Super Hornets or the F-35. It is also unlikely to matter much to the Americans either. Indeed, US North Command is now advocating for slower and lighter fighters - a telling sign that the Americans themselves are not necessarily convinced on the threat posed by advanced Russian aircraft.

With most of our key allies poised to purchase the Joint Strike Fighter, Canada's capacity to continue participating in aerial combat operations abroad is also clearly at issue. Indeed, critics of the purchase have been quick to highlight this expeditionary role as being the true *raison d' être* for the F-35. In the colourful words of Steven Staples of the Rideau Institute, this aircraft is a "first-strike fighter-bomber" that will be used "in the first wave of aircraft screaming over the beaches to bomb cities and military bases on the first night of war."

There is certainly some truth to this statement. The F-35's stealth technology and advanced weapon systems would prove especially useful for the suppression of an adversary's air defence and to secure air superiority over the battlefield. At the very least, stealth technology will prove useful as a means to maximize the survivability of the aircraft in hostile environments. With the spread of advanced aircraft and air defence systems, the Super Hornet - unlike the F-35 - might simply find itself too vulnerable to attack. This does not mean that these jets would be unable to participate. But it might be unwise to place such an aircraft in a hostile combat environment - and the United States, always keen to maximize operational efficiency, may simply not accept such a contribution in the first place or relegate them to a token role in the aftermath of the initial air campaign

True, Canada has not participated in an air war since the 1999 Kosovo War. And there is certainly a great degree of discretion in whether Canada participates in such operations and the nature of that contribution itself. But it would be wrong-headed to assume that expeditionary operations will only be limited to counter-insurgency missions in undeveloped fragile states. Canada might very well find itself participating in combat operations against a more advanced state with sophisticated air defence and anti-access capabilities. And without the F-35 to contribute, Canada might in turn find itself sending significant naval or ground forces to compensate.

The decision to acquire the F-35 seems unnecessary from a domestic and continental perspective. But with its stealth technology and advanced weapon/network systems, these fighters are more appropriate if Canada is to continue to fully participate in air combat operations abroad. In that sense, it certainly fits with Canada's long-standing policy - spelled out in various defence white papers and statements - to maintain a "multi-purpose combat capable force" able to fight "alongside the best, against the best."

Yet one should also not be complacent with such important matters. Indeed, it might be prudent for the government to more fully re-assess the role of the air force and the need to contribute its air force for high-intensity combat missions. The F-35, while having the requisite capabilities for such operations, might simply be too expensive a choice for the Canadian military. And if this means that Canada might no longer be capable of participating in a coalition air war, perhaps it is now finally time to seriously look at that option.

A more specialized role for our air force, focused more on domestic and continental tasks with the acquisition of the cheaper Super Hornet, might appear to be a risky proposition. But given the need for fiscal restraint and soaring costs of advanced weapon platforms, the status quo is not without danger. Simply put, the decision to acquire the F-35s can easily result in significant opportunity costs. For example, the navy could find little funds available in the capital budget when its major surface combatants are in need of replacement.

Canadian governments generally prefer to avoid making hard choices on defence. However, with the recent F-35 controversy and major naval procurement projects on the horizon, it is perhaps finally time for the government to begin to take a hard look at and make some difficult decisions on the future of Canadian defence policy, force structure and procurement priorities.

David S. McDonough is a Doctoral Candidate at Dalhousie University, a Doctoral Fellow at Dalhousie's Centre for Foreign Policy Studies, and is presently a Visiting Research Associate at the Centre for International Policy Studies, University of Ottawa. He is the editor of the CIC-CDFAI Strategic Studies Working Group's forthcoming book, Canada's National Security in the Post-9/11 World: Strategy, Interests and Threats. *He would like to thank Philippe Lagassé for helpful comments on an earlier draft of this commentary.*

UK Will Not Decide F-35 Numbers Before 2015

By Rhys Jones and Mohammed Abbas/Reuters
LONDON

Britain has deferred to 2015 a firm commitment on how many Lockheed Martin F-35 Joint Strike Fighters it will buy, adding to uncertainties over the multinational program which has recently been questioned in the U.S. Congress.

"We will not make final decisions on the overall number of aircraft we will order before the next planned Strategic Defense Review (in 2015)," a Defense Ministry spokeswoman said Feb. 7, adding an initial order would be placed next year.

The F-35 project ranks as the most expensive U.S. arms program but has been criticized for cost overruns at a time when next week's U.S. fiscal 2013 budget plan is expected to postpone funding for 179 warplanes until after 2017—a move that has prompted international partners to question their own procurement plans.

Britain in 2001 committed to buy 138 of the multirole stealth aircraft, but the current coalition government in its 2010 defense review said it would cut the number of F-35s it had on order without saying by how many.

Britain has so far placed a firm order with Lockheed for three F-35 test and evaluation aircraft costing $632 million.

A spokesman for Lockheed, the top U.S. defense contractor, said Britain's total order had not been revised down and remained at 138. Britain was due to receive its first F-35 in June.

Other partners in the project include Canada, Denmark, the Netherlands and Norway.

While there have been reports Britain will cut its order to 50 F-35s, the Defense Ministry said it did not recognize that figure. Expectations for the number of F-35s Britain will eventually order have been curtailed since the ministry's decision to use only one aircraft carrier, which will routinely have 12 fast jets embarked for operations, while retaining a capacity to deploy up to 36.

In the U.S., cuts to the F-35 program are part of the Pentagon's plan to start implementing $487 billion in defense spending reductions over the next decade.

ANNEX 5

JSF Press Release, 16 July 2010

Government Of Canada Strengthens Sovereignty While Generating Significant Economic Benefits
NR - 10.079 - July 16, 2010

OTTAWA – The Government of Canada today announced it is acquiring the fifth generation Joint Strike Fighter F-35 aircraft to contribute to the modernization of the Canadian Forces, while bringing significant economic benefits and opportunities to regions across Canada.

"The F-35 Joint Strike Fighter is the best aircraft we can provide our men and women in uniform to face and defeat the challenges of the 21st century," said the Honourable Peter MacKay, Minister of National Defence. "This multi-role stealth fighter will help the Canadian Forces defend the sovereignty of Canadian airspace, remain a strong and reliable partner in the defence of North America, and provide Canada with an effective and modern capability for international operations."

"A lengthy and intense competition was completed in 2001 for who would build the F-35," said the Honourable Rona Ambrose, Minister of Public Works and Government Services and Minister for Status of Women. "Canadian companies and the Canadian government helped develop the F-35, and now we are exercising our option under the Joint Strike Fighter memorandum of understanding to acquire it."

"Canadian participation in the Joint Strike Fighter program will bring high-value jobs and other economic benefits to our country," said Jacques Gourde, Parliamentary Secretary to the Minister of Public Works and Government Services and to the Minister of National Revenue and Member of Parliament for Lotbinière-Chutes-de-la-Chaudière. "This government is delivering on our plan to strengthen Canada's defence industry, leverage Canada's competitive advantage and work with industry to help position Canadian companies for success in the global marketplace."

The Government of Canada has committed approximately $9 billion to the acquisition of 65 F-35 aircraft and associated weapons, infrastructure, initial spares, training simulators, contingency funds and project operating costs. Delivery of the new aircraft is expected to start in 2016.

To date, Canada has invested approximately $168 million in the Joint Strike Fighter program. Since 2002, the Government's participation in the program has led to more than $350 million in contracts for more than 85 Canadian companies, research laboratories, and universities – a clear demonstration of the significant benefits this program has for Canada.

"The Joint Strike Fighter program allows Canadian companies to build on existing strengths and establish strategic capabilities," said the Honourable Tony Clement, Minister of Industry. "Canadian companies will have direct involvement in the design of equipment in the short term, while also setting in motion opportunities for decades to come."

The Canada First Defence Strategy identifies Canada's need for a next generation fighter aircraft to protect the safety and security of Canadians, while supporting foreign policy and national security objectives. The acquisition of the F-35 helps the Canadian Forces defend against the threats of the 21st century at home, across vast distances and in harsh environmental conditions, and abroad.

The F-35 Lightning II has been developed by Lockheed Martin and partners through the Joint Strike Fighter program, a multinational effort to build and sustain an affordable, multi-role, next generation stealth fighter aircraft. Canada, the United States, the United Kingdom, the Netherlands, Italy, Turkey, Denmark, Norway, and Australia are all partners in the program.

As a partner in the Joint Strike Fighter program since 1997, Canada participated in the extensive and rigorous US-led competitive process, which led to the selection of Lockheed Martin and its partners as the Joint Strike Fighter manufacturer in 2001.

ANNEX 6

Interview with Lt.-Gen. Andre Deschamps

The air force must plan for the CF-18's replacement soon

The CP 140 has had some upgrades but DND will need to think about a replacement soon

as I had hoped for this year. I think everything is in place now for us to hit our stride, from the instructors, the amount of airplanes, and the technology in place to truly support a highly productive pilot system.

BEST PILOT TRAINING IN THE WORLD

I feel we have the best pilot training system in the world. It is resource intensive, but it produces top notch folks, and the same can be said of our technicians. I can point to proof of that in the success of how quickly we went to the Chinook Delta [CH-47D] for operation in Afghanistan. From the government decision to use the aircraft, to having it deployed and operating was eight months. The reason we were able to go so quickly is because we invest a lot in our training, we have high quality technicians, they are very adaptable, and the same goes for our aircrew. I'm pretty certain that's why we were able to go into that new domain so cold, and yet be so successful.

CDR: What is planned for the Chinook Delta fleet once we leave Afghanistan?
CAS: I've made some recommendations to government based on what we see as our needs back home once we leave Afghanistan, and I'm waiting for a decision. Clearly we see the Chinook Foxtrot as our next focus from a training and operation perspective. The Delta's have been tremendous and they're still doing great work. They are an absolute workhorse and a wonderful airplane. What happens to them after we leave Afghanistan is mostly a resource and money discussion, but I think we've made some reasonable suggestions to government and we'll see which way they want to go.

NEXT GEN FIGHTER

CDR: Where is the next generation fighter on your list of priorities?
CAS: The next generation fighter is very high on my list. We know government wants to get to that discussion soon, and we definitely need to get on with a process to get a new fighter. It sounds like a long time away, but as we know it takes a lot to go through a contracting process and produce a new fighter. We just finished upgrading our CF-18s to what we call the R2 standard. It's a tremendous upgrade creating a great platform, and will give us a high performing aircraft to keep us competitive certainly through this decade. That doesn't mean we shouldn't move forward on selecting what will replace the CF-18. We're moving forward hopefully in the not too distant future to establish a discussion with government.

There's also a lot of other procurement that we still need to resolve. The Fixed-Wing Search and Rescue replacement is probably the one we need to get through, but the replacement of the CP-140 is the next discussion after we get through the fighter discussion. We have great plans and we have time to make those decisions as we're certainly not in a panic on any of those fronts right now, but we definitely need to get to those discussions with government so we can have a good plan to move on at the end of this decade.

CDR: Thank you. ∎

ANNEX 7

AIT

Article 506.11 of the AIT states that:

An entity of a Party may use procurement procedures that are different from those described in paragraphs 1 through 10 in the following circumstances provided that it does not do so for the purpose of avoiding competition between suppliers or in order to discriminate again supplies of any other Party:

(a) where an unforeseeable situation of urgency exists and the goods, services or construction cannot be obtained in time by means of open procurement procedures;

(b) where goods or consulting services regarding matters of a confidential or privileged nature are to be purchased and the disclosure of those matters through an open tendering process could reasonably be expected to compromise government confidentiality, cause economic disruption or otherwise be contrary to the public interest;

(c) where a contract is to be awarded under a cooperation agreement that is financed, in whole or in part, by an international cooperation organization, only to the extent that the agreement between the Party and the organization includes rules for awarding contracts that differ from the obligations set out in this Chapter;

(d) where construction materials are to be purchased and it can be demonstrated that transportation costs or technical considerations impose geographic limits on the available supply base, specifically in the case of sand, stone, gravel, asphalt compound and pre-mixed concrete for use in the construction or repair of roads;

(e) where compliance with the open tendering provisions set out in this Chapter would interfere with a Party's ability to maintain security or order or to protect human, animal or plant life or health; and

(f) in the absence of a receipt of any bids in response to a call for tenders made in accordance with the procedures set out in this Chapter.

Article 506.12 of the AIT states:

Where only one supplier is able to meet the requirements of procurement, an entity may use procurement procedures that are different from those described in paragraphs one through ten in the following circumstances:

(a) to ensure compatibility with existing products, to recognize exclusive rights, such as exclusive licenses, copyright and patent rights, or to maintain specialized products that must be maintained by the manufacturer or its representative;

(b) where there is an absence of competition for technical reasons and the goods or services can be supplied only by a particular supplier and no alternative or substitute exists;

(c) for the procurement of goods or services the supply of which is controlled by a supplier that is a statutory monopoly;

(d) for the purchase of goods on a commodity market;

(e) for work to be performed on or about a leased building or portions thereof that may be performed only by the lessor;

(f) for work to be performed on property by a contractor according to provisions of a warranty or guarantee held in respect of the property or the original work;

(g) for a contract to be awarded to the winner of a design contest;

(h) for the procurement of a prototype or a first good or service to be developed in the course of and for a particular contract for research, experiment, study or original development, but not for any subsequent purchases;

(i) for the purchase of goods under exceptionally advantageous circumstances such as bankruptcy or receivership, but not for routine purchases;

(j) for the procurement of original works of art;

(k) for the procurement of subscriptions to newspapers, magazines or other periodicals; and

(l) for the procurement of property.

National Security

Article 1804 of the AIT reads as follows:

> Nothing in this Agreement shall be construed to:
>
> (a) require the federal government to provide, or allow access to, information the disclosure of which it determines to be contrary to national security; or
>
> (b) prevent the federal government from taking any action that it considers necessary to protect national security interests or, pursuant to its international obligations, for the maintenance of international peace and security.

ANNEX 8

Extracts from Treasury Board Contracting Policy

TB Contracting Policy

10.2 Exceptions

10.2.1 Section 6 of the *Government Contracts Regulations* contains four exceptions that permit the contracting authority to set aside the requirement to solicit bids. These are:

a. the need is one of pressing emergency in which delay would be injurious to the public interest;

b. the estimated expenditure does not exceed
   - $25,000,
   - $100,000, where the contract is for the acquisition of architectural, engineering and other services required in respect of the planning, design, preparation or supervision of the construction, repair, renovation or restoration of a work, or
   - $100,000 where the contract is to be entered into by the member of the Queen's Privy Council for Canada responsible for the Canadian International Development Agency and is for the acquisition of architectural, engineering or other services required in respect of the planning, design, preparation or supervision of an international development assistance program or project;

c. the nature of the work is such that it would not be in the public interest to solicit bids; or

d. only one person or firm is capable of performing the contract.

10.2.2 In exception (a), a pressing emergency is a situation where delay in taking action would be injurious to the public interest. Emergencies are normally unavoidable and require immediate action which would preclude the solicitation of formal bids. An emergency may be an actual or imminent life-threatening situation, a disaster which endangers the quality of life or has resulted in the loss of life, or one that may result in significant loss or damage to Crown property.

10.2.3 Exception (b) sets specific dollar limits below which a contracting authority may set aside the competitive process. However, contracting authorities are expected to call for bids whenever it is cost effective to do so. When the proposed contract is estimated to exceed the dollar limits, the contracting authority is to call for bids.

10.2.4 Exception (c) should normally be reserved for dealing with security considerations or to alleviate some significant socio-economic disparity. For example, the preservation of a certain source of supply may be necessary to ensure that future needs of government can be met. This exception should be invoked only with the approval of senior management as delegated by the contracting authority (the minister).

10.2.5 Exception (d) sets competitive bidding aside when only one person or firm can do the job. This exception is quite definitive and should be invoked only where patent or copyright requirements, or technical compatibility factors and technological expertise suggest that only one contractor exists. This exception should not be invoked simply because a proposed contractor is the only one known to management.

10.2.6 Any use of the four exceptions to the bidding requirement should be fully justified on the contract file or, where applicable, in submissions to the Treasury Board. Even if a proposed directed contract (see Appendix A) for goods and services qualifies under one of these four exceptions, the contracting authority is encouraged, whenever possible, to use the electronic bidding methodology to advertise the proposed award through an Advance Contract Award Notice (ACAN). If no statements of capabilities meeting the requirements set out in the ACAN are received within fifteen calendar days, the proposed contract is deemed to be competitive and may be awarded using the electronic bidding contracting authority.

Should the contracting authority have to seek the Treasury Board's approval to award such a contract, it should be noted that the Treasury Board cannot approve a directed contract which does not meet at least one of the four exceptions. In such cases, an exception to the Regulations by means of an Order In Council would be required.

(link: http://www.tbs-sct.gc.ca/pol/doc-eng.aspx?id=14494&section=text)

ANNEX 9

Briefing Note – September 2006

RELEASED UNDER AIA. INFORMATION UNCLASSIFIED
DIVULGUÉ EN VERTU DE LA LAI RENSEIGNEMENTS NON CLASSIFIÉS

s.13(1)(a)
s.15(1)
s.21(1)(b)

SD Sep 06

BRIEFING NOTE FOR THE MINISTER

JSF PROGRAM

ISSUE

1. The purpose of this briefing note is to provide an update to the Minister of National Defence regarding Canada's current activities on the Joint Strike Fighter (JSF) program.

BACKGROUND

2. The JSF ~~[redacted]~~ role next generation ~~[redacted]~~ program with nine international participants including the United States, Italy, the United Kingdom, Norway, Denmark, Australia, the Netherlands, Turkey and Canada.

3. JSF will be the single largest fighter aircraft program of the first half of the 21st Century, with a total estimated program value in excess of $270B USD. Three versions of the aircraft will be built: conventional takeoff and landing (CTOL); carrier version (CV); and short takeoff and vertical landing (STOVL). Total partnership and export sales are expected to top 5000 aircraft. Canada is currently considering the CTOL version of the aircraft. Canada has been a participant in the JSF program since 1997.

4. In 2002, Canada joined the System Development and Demonstration Phase (SDD) with an investment of $150M USD. In the SDD phase, Industry Canada contributed $50M USD to support JSF related R&D efforts involving Canadian industry. The same arrangement is not possible in the PSFD phase as the requirement is for direct financial contributions only. The SDD phase runs through 2013.

5. In 2003, the United States invited the current partners to participate in the Production, Sustainment and Follow-On Development (PSFD) phase of the program. The draft PSFD MOU text was finalized among the partners in June 2006. The cost for Canada to participate in the next phase would be approximately   spread over the period   This contribution would be used to cover Canada's portion of PSFD costs including;

It should be noted that participation in the PSFD phase of the program does not commit any partner to procure aircraft and that all partners are permitted to withdraw from the MOU at anytime.

DISCUSSION

6. In May 2006, CAS completed an options analysis study that examined the global market for next-generation tactical fighter aircraft. The results of this study have indicated that the JSF family of aircraft provides the best available operational

RELEASED UNDER AIA. INFORMATION UNCLASSIFIED
DIVULGUÉ EN VERTU DE LA LAI RENSEIGNEMENTS NON CLASSIFIÉS(1)(a)

s.15(1)
s.20(1)(c)
s.21(1)(b)
s.69(1)

capabilities to meet Canadian operational requirements, while providing the longest service life and the lowest per aircraft cost of all options considered
    A decision regarding the replacement of the CF-18 will be sought in   At that time, DND will have spent approximately $129.3M USD towards participation in the PSFD phase of the JSF program.

8.

9.

10.   DND's participation in the JSF program is widely supported by Canadian Industry and OGDs such as, IC, FAC and ITC. To date Canadian industry has secured approximately 150 JSF contracts with an estimated value of $157M USD. Canada's continued participation would result in an estimated additional   in industrial opportunities starting in 2007.

11.   On 19 July 2006, participation in the PSFD MOU was approved by the PMB.

WAY AHEAD

12.

Prepared by: Sara Domina, DCMC, 996-7126
Responsible Group Principal: Mr. Dan Ross, ADM(Mat), 992-6622
Date: 19 September 2006

ANNEX 10

"UK, Canada Keep JSF Options Open"

U.K., Canada Keep JSF Options Open

Insidedefense.com NewsStand | Carlo Munoz | December 16, 2006

Even though Pentagon officials this week inked agreements with three of the eight Joint Strike Fighter partner nations, two of those countries will continue to examine secondary options to the F-35 in the coming months, international defense officials tell *Inside the Air Force*.

Representatives from the United States, Canada, Australia and the United Kingdom all approved an international memorandum of understanding solidifying the participation of those nations for the next stage of development on the fifth-generation aircraft.

The MOU is expected to lay out a set of principles that will formally articulate the international fighter effort's production schedule. It also is expected to cover sustainment and follow-on development issues for the multibillion-dollar program, according to U.S. defense officials.

Perhaps more importantly, the MOU could dictate terms and an overall number of component and system transfers that would be granted to the U.S. allies participating in the F-35 program.

U.S. and Canadian defense officials finalized terms of the MOU during a Dec. 11 signing ceremony at the Pentagon. Representatives from the U.K. and Australian defense ministries followed suit a day later, ratifying the terms of the MOU during separate ceremonies at the Pentagon and the State Department, respectively.

Noting the effort "has proved to us to be an excellent program [and] an excellent example of international cooperation and collaboration," Canada's Joint Strike Fighter program manager, Michael Slack, said his nation is pleased with the final version of the agreement.

"At the end of the day, we reached a consensus on what was going to be required by Canada to operate and sustain these airplanes well into the future," he said during a Dec. 11 interview.

ITAF first reported in July that representatives from each of the participating nations signed a draft version of the MOU. Since that time, defense officials in each country turned their focus toward garnering approval of the pact's language within their respective governments.

For its part, the United Kingdom viewed the MOU as a "very important and positive" outcome, after months of formal and informal negotiations between the two allies, personal assurances from senior U.S. defense

U.K., Canada Keep JSF Options Open

officials and a contentious debate regarding the transfer of sensitive technology information, U.K. procurement czar Lord Drayson said.

"I wasn't sure that we were going to get there . . . [but] this is an important stepping stone" for the continued participation of the United Kingdom on the F-35 project, Drayson said during a Dec. 12 press conference in Washington, following the signing of the multinational development pact.

International JSF members have argued for increased access to developing technologies related to the F-35, so they can adequately perform mandatory maintenance and sustainment work through the life of the aircraft, defense sources say.

Earlier this year, Drayson told members of the Senate Armed Services Committee that the United Kingdom would pull out of the F-35 coalition due to a perceived unwillingness by the Pentagon to disclose sensitive technological information.

More recently, a Dec. 8 report issued by a key defense committee in the U.K. House of Commons suggested that the Ministry of Defence "switch a majority of its efforts" toward a "Plan B" alternatives to the F-35, should the U.S. continue to deny full disclosure of sensitive technologies.

But after an intense round of last-minute negotiations, coupled with a personal assurance from U.S. acquisition czar Kenneth Krieg that the U.S. would accommodate their demands for "operational sovereignty" on the F-35, the United Kingdom agreed to the terms in the MOU.

To that end, Defense Department officials also inked individual agreements with Canada and Australia regarding technology transfer issues, senior military officials from those countries told *ITAF*.

With the Netherlands signing the international procurement pact in November, the remaining JSF coalition members who have yet to sign are Italy, Turkey, Denmark and Norway.

Even with technology transfer issues resolved, the United Kingdom still plans to explore alternatives to the F-35 under the "Plan B" strategy, outlined by the Parliamentary defence panel, Drayson said.

Refusing to go into details regarding those Plan B options, the U.K.'s procurement chief said his government has repeatedly emphasized the importance of seeking F-35 alternatives.

The JSF "provides the military capability we need . . . but it is absolutely right for the United Kingdom to have a plan B," he said during the Dec. 12 briefing.

While echoing the sentiment that preliminary evaluations of the F-35 have shown the aircraft to be the answer to its fighter requirements, Canadian defense officials are also looking at potential alternatives to the fifth-generation aircraft.

"I think that we are going to look at the full spectrum of capabilities to meet future operational requirements," Slack said in the interview. "If something emerges that turns out to be extremely capable, who knows? I do not have a crystal ball anymore than you do."

Canadian defense officials are eying the 2012 time frame for a final decision on what platform, or mix of platforms, will replace the F/A-18E/F Super Hornets that make up the majority of Canada's fighter fleet.

U.K., Canada Keep JSF Options Open

Production aircraft seen as possible alternatives to the JSF include the JAS 39 Gripen and the Eurofighter Typhoon, along with upgraded versions of the Super Hornet, Col. Dave Burt, Canada's director for air requirements, said in a brief Dec. 11 interview with *ITAF*.

That eventual fighter force structure is expected to be transitioned into the Canadian air force between 2017 and 2020, he added.

However, the chances of Canada fielding a mixed fighter fleet are slim, Burt said, adding that the operation and sustainment costs to field two fighter platforms would be too expensive.

"We will look at all options, but from an affordability perspective, that would create significant challenges," Burt said. "Having a mixed fleet, in relatively small numbers, would be extremely expensive."

The more likely option would be to select a single fighter aircraft to fill the country's requirements, he added.

Earlier this year, military officials from JSF partner nation Norway began their own "concept solution study," evaluating military requirements and the capabilities provided by the JSF and other similar aircraft.

The study covers a wide spectrum of options -- from modifying the nation's current fleet of F-16s with state-of-the-art systems to fielding a new mixed fleet composed of F-35s and a second fighter, Norwegian Defense Attache Maj. Gen Tom Knutsen said during a brief interview at a Sept. 6 international interoperability seminar in Washington.

Noting the examination of F-35 alternatives probably will not result in any one country leaving the program, Burt said the exploratory efforts were simply geared toward learning what exactly the fighter has to offer, outside the issues relating to the MOU.

"Up until this point . . . a very large part of Canada's program has been about industrial issues and [technology] transfer issues" in the MOU, Burt said. "We have done a relatively modest operational analysis" of this program, he added.

ANNEX 11

APA Stealth Analysis

Mr Secretary - Why Does the Pentagon Say the JSF is a 5th Generation Fighter . . Really?

Air Power Australia - Australia's Independent Defence Think Tank

Air Power Australia NOTAM
8th November, 2009

Peter Goon, BEng (Mech), FTE (USNTPS),
Head of Test and Evaluation, Air Power Australia

Contacts: Peter Goon   Carlo Kopp
            Mob: 0419-806-476   Mob: 0437-478-224

JOINT STRIKE FIGHTER – INHERENT LIMITATIONS

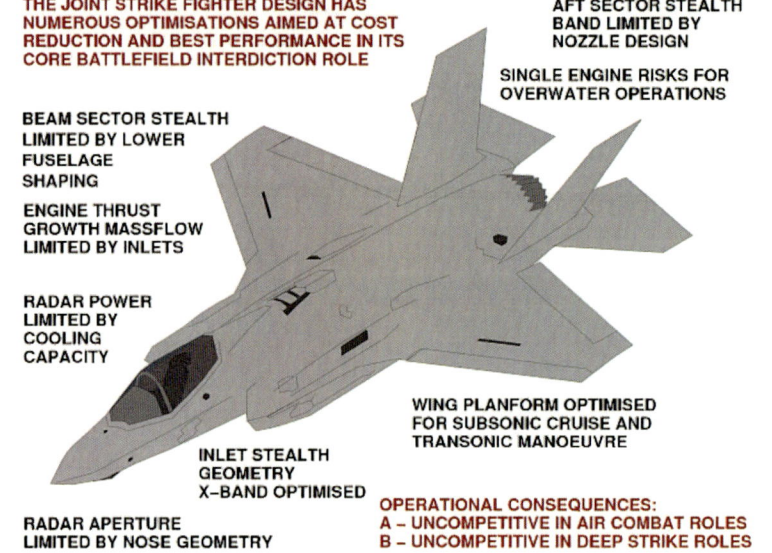

THE JOINT STRIKE FIGHTER DESIGN HAS NUMEROUS OPTIMISATIONS AIMED AT COST REDUCTION AND BEST PERFORMANCE IN ITS CORE BATTLEFIELD INTERDICTION ROLE

AFT SECTOR STEALTH BAND LIMITED BY NOZZLE DESIGN

SINGLE ENGINE RISKS FOR OVERWATER OPERATIONS

BEAM SECTOR STEALTH LIMITED BY LOWER FUSELAGE SHAPING

ENGINE THRUST GROWTH MASSFLOW LIMITED BY INLETS

RADAR POWER LIMITED BY COOLING CAPACITY

WING PLANFORM OPTIMISED FOR SUBSONIC CRUISE AND TRANSONIC MANOEUVRE

INLET STEALTH GEOMETRY X-BAND OPTIMISED

RADAR APERTURE LIMITED BY NOSE GEOMETRY

OPERATIONAL CONSEQUENCES:
A – UNCOMPETITIVE IN AIR COMBAT ROLES
B – UNCOMPETITIVE IN DEEP STRIKE ROLES

THESE DESIGN LIMITATIONS CANNOT BE CHANGED BY UPGRADES

To: The Hon Robert Gates
US Secretary of Defense

Dear Mr Gates,

The term *5th Generation Fighter* appears very frequently these days in public statements, press releases, PowerPoint slides and interviews. More than often the label is attached concurrently to the F-35 Lightning II Joint Strike Fighter and the F-22A Raptor, despite the enormous differences in the design of these aircraft.

This begs two very basic questions. What is a *5th Generation fighter*; and which fighters actually qualify as *5th Generation* designs? The question which follows, is whether the F-35 Lightning II Joint Strike Fighter actually qualifies, on merit, as a *5th Generation fighter*.

APA decided to test the evidence, and using data and facts from robust sources, compiled a comparison matrix to tease out what capabilities, features and attributes define a 5th Generation fighter design.

To score the candidate aircraft, the APA proprietary Zero-One Comparative Tabulation (ZOCT) technique, which assigns normalised scores against clearly defined measures is used; namely:

-1 Does not meet a Fifth Generation Air Dominance Fighter metric
 0 Capability meets a Fifth Generation Air Dominance Fighter metric
+1 Enhanced Capability meets a Fifth Generation Air Dominance Fighter metric

Though some interpretation on any skew induced by the specifics of particular metrics and their relations with other capability metrics may be necessary, in general:

- A total score of Zero (0) signifies the candidate aircraft meets the criteria for categorisation as a Fifth Generation Fighter.

- A total score greater than Zero (0), i.e. a total positive score, signifies the same but denotes there are enhancing characteristics. The larger the positive score, the more the candidate aircraft may be referred to as an Advanced Fifth Generation Fighter Aircraft.

- A total score that is negative indicates the candidate aircraft does not meet the criteria for being called a Fifth Generation Fighter. The larger the negative score, the further away the candidate aircraft is from being able to be called a Fifth Generation Fighter.

The JSF achieving a total score of minus eight (-8) assessed across these 14 capability metrics would appear to leave only one - self evident - conclusion to be drawn.

That this contrivance is not in the best interests of our Nations or those of other friends who, in good faith, agreed to participate in the JSF Program, is also self evident, stemming from the same 'total indifference to reality' that gave us the Global Financial Crisis and its more rapacious emerging offspring, the World Economic Realignment.

That the JSF Program needs fixing is not in doubt. How this may best be achieved is well understood by the international team of experts at Air Power Australia, whose advice has, to date, been ignored by most of those who advise you.

As ever, this small group of dedicated and diligent citizens remain willing and able to assist in doing what is right and what is best for our Nations and those of our friends.

Yours sincerely,

Peter Goon
Peter Goon
Principal Consultant/Adviser
Head of Test and Evaluation
Co-Founder, Air Power Australia
Peter Goon and Associates

Mob: +61 (0)41 980 6476
Sunday, 8 November 2009

IS THE JSF REALLY A FIFTH GENERATION FIGHTER?

5th Generation Fighter Capabilities	Modern Fighters				Current Threat	
	F-22A Raptor	T-50 PAK-FA	J-12/J-XX	F-35 JSF Lightning II	Gen 4++ Su-35S	
	USA	Russia	China	International	Russia	
Super Cruise	Yes > 1.7 Mach (0)	2.0 Mach Design Target (+1)	Yes (0)	No (-1)	Yes (0)	
High Agility Supersonic/ Subsonic	Yes (0)	Extreme Agility (+1)	Yes (0)	Neither (-1)	Extreme Agility (+1)	
High Specific Excess Power - P_s	Yes (0)	Yes (0)	Yes (0)	No (-1)	Yes (0)	
Thrust Vectoring Control - TVC	Yes 2-D (0)	Yes 3-D (+1)	Yes (0)	No (-1)	Yes 3-D (+1)	
Highly Integrated Avionics	Yes (0)	Yes (0)	Yes (0)	Yes (0)	Yes (0)	
Electronically Steered Array (ESA) Radar	High Power Aperture (+1)	High Power Aperture (+1)	Yes (0)	Medium Power Aperture (0)	High Power Aperture (+1)	
Sidelooking ESA Apertures	Fitted For But Not With (FFBNW) (0)	Yes (+1)	Unknown	No (-1)	Yes (0)	
High Situational Awareness (SA) - Onboard/Offboard	Yes (0)	Yes (0)	Likely	Yes (0)	Yes (0)	
Supersonic Weapons Delivery	Yes (0)	Yes (0)	Yes (0)	No (Bomber Doors) (-1	Yes (0)	
Large Thrust to Weight Multi Engine Thrust Growth	Yes 2 Engines Large Growth (0)	Yes 2 Engines Large Growth (0)	Yes 2 Engines Large Growth (0)	Middling T/W One Engine Little Growth (-1)	Yes 2 Engines Large Growth (0)	
High Combat Ceiling (> 7 deg/sec turn rate, sustained)	Yes > 55 kft (0)	Yes > 55 kft (0)	Yes > 50 kft (0)	No < 45 kft (-1)	Yes > 55 kft (0)	

Very Low Observable Stealth/ Low Observables	All Aspect, Wideband (+1)	All Aspect, Wideband Design Target (0)	Yes or Partial (0)	Yes but Partial (0)	No (-1)
Large Internal Fuel Load lbs	Yes >18 klbs (0)	Yes >20 klbs (0)	Unknown	Yes >18 klbs (0)	Yes >25 klbs (+1)
Internal Weapon Carriage Hard Point Stations	Yes 6 + 2 (0)	Yes 8 - 10 (0)	Highly Likely Nos. Unknown (0)	Yes 4 (0)	Partial (Tunnel Pod) 2 - 4 (-1)
ZOCT Scoring by 5th Gen Metrics	+2	+5	0	-8	+2

Table © 2009, Peter Goon, Air Power Australia, Peter Goon & Associates.

Air Power Australia Website - http://www.ausairpower.net/
Air Power Australia Research and Analysis - http://www.ausairpower.net/research.html

ANNEX 12

"F-35 Defeated in Air Combat Simulation"

F-35 Lightning II News
F-35 defeated in air combat simulation

September 7, 2011 (by Eric L. Palmer) - **F-16.net has learned from an unnamed source, that earlier this year a presentation was given by an industry air combat threat assessment expert to defense officials of a NATO country which showed that the F-35 Joint Strike Fighter (JSF) would not survive air combat against threats it is likely to see in its alleged service lifetime.**

Part of the presentation showed a computer simulation which calculated that the F-35 would be consistently defeated by the Russian-made SU-35 fighter aircraft. The defeat calculated by the scenario also showed the loss of the F-35's supporting airborne-early warning and air-to-air refueling aircraft.

USAF F-35A #08-7046, the third production model of the F-35 Lightning II, completed its inaugural flight on May 6th, 2011 from NAS Fort Worth with Lockheed Martin test pilot Bill Gigliotti at the controls.

The technology in the SU-35 will also see its way into growth upgrades of other SU-fighter variants used by countries like Indonesia, India, Malaysia and Vietnam. Chinese variants of these aircraft should also see similar growth capability in the coming years.

The Russian-made T-50, PAK-FA low-observable fighter now in development is expected to be much more lethal than the SU-35 in air-to-air combat against the U.S. made F-35. The SU-35 and T-50 made appearances this year at the Russian aerospace industry air show known as MAKS2011. Both aircraft will include sensors and networking which can minimise the effects of the limited low-observable qualities of the F-35. They will also have higher performance and carry more air-to-air weapons than an F-35.

The F-35 defeat briefing runs counter to the claims by the Lockheed Martin corporation that the F-35 will be a go-it-alone aircraft in high threat situations (brief to Israel, 2007) or that it will be "8 times" more effective than "legacy" aircraft in air-to-air combat.

In 2009, then U.S. Secretary of Defense Mr. Gates was successful in halting additional production of the F-22 which is the only aircraft that can take on emerging threats. His reasoning was that the F-35—built in numbers—would be sufficient to fill any strategic gaps in air power deterrence for the U.S. and its allies.

There was never any robust strategic study performed by the U.S. Department of Defense to verify Gates theory.

Since Gates endorsement of the troubled F-35 program, it has continued with its history of cost blow-outs and delay and is unlikely to see a large number built.

If Gates is wrong, he will have helped put the the air power deterrent capability of the U.S. and its allies at significant risk in the coming years. According to the assumptions of the joint operational requirement of the F-35 signed off on in 2000, the F-35 was not supposed to take on high-end threats. The requirement assumed that there would be hundreds of combat-ready F-22s. With the F-22 program ending, the maximum number of combat-ready F-22s will be somewhere between 120 and 140.

Independent air combat analysts from Air Power Australia have also stated that the F-35 is not capable of facing high end threats; that what will be delivered (if it ever arrives) will be obsolete; and that the F-35 is not affordable or sustainable.

A recent briefing by Australian Defence officials, while showing support for the F-35 program, admitted that it will cost more to operate than the F-18 Hornet. A separate U.S. Navy study also agreed. This is counter to the claim by Lockheed Martin, that the F-35 will be cheaper to operate than existing aircraft it is planned to replace.

In 2012, Australian Defence will decide to put down money for its first order of F-35s or to go ahead with a "plan-B" that could include purchase of 24 more F-18 Super Hornets made by Boeing. The Super Hornet is also unable to take on high-end threats in the Pacific Rim region in the coming years.

ANNEX 13

Boeing's Cost Estimates for the Super Hornet

From: ALLAN DEQUETTEVILLE <adequetteville@rogers.com>
To: alan WILLIAMS <williamsgroup@rogers.com>
Sent: Thursday, October 6, 2011 7:44:09 AM
Subject: Re: cost?

Alan

Boeing folks have confirmed your assessment of Super Hornet costs is correct.

From: alan WILLIAMS <williamsgroup@rogers.com>
To: ALLAN DEQUETTEVILLE <adequetteville@rogers.com>
Sent: Monday, October 3, 2011 5:41:45 PM
Subject: Re: cost?

Thanks. If I read the material correctly, for fiscal year 2011, Boeing's recurring unit cost is $54.9 million (vs. F-35 $75+ million) and the average procurement cost is $83 million ($1.828 billion divided by 22) (vs F-35 $110+ million). Correct?

Alan

From: ALLAN DEQUETTEVILLE <adequetteville@rogers.com>
To: alan WILLIAMS <williamsgroup@rogers.com>
Sent: Monday, October 3, 2011 4:55:51 PM
Subject: Re: cost?

Alan

Here is the input I got from the SH Program in St Louis.......you may note that the "current multi-year contract with the USN" was what Kory Matthews referred to at Parliamentary hearing last Nov.......probably more than you wanted, but for sake of completeness I have included the ref attachments:

A go-to-war Super Hornet costs approximately $54M in CY-10 dollars, under the current multi-year contract with the US Navy. This includes: engines; APG-79 AESA radar; all avionics, EW Suite; ATFLIR, armament; external fuel tanks and JHMCS.

Looking at attachment "SH cost" which is taken from the "Department of the Navy Fiscal Year (FY) 2012 Budget Estimates" P-40 document; the Super Hornet runs between $55-57M USD, even with estimated changes (Rec Flyaway ECO) of ~$1M per a/c included.

Attachment "APN_BA1-4" is the entire USN FY2012 budget document. This document can be used to compare Super Hornet to F35 numbers. All are public access documents on the USN website.

Cheers

Al

From: alan WILLIAMS <williamsgroup@rogers.com>
To: ALLAN DEQUETTEVILLE <adequetteville@rogers.com>
Sent: Saturday, October 1, 2011 8:26:01 PM
Subject: cost?

Al could you give me a rough ballpark as to what is the cost of a Super Hornet? Thanks.

Alan

ANNEX 14

PBO Cost Estimate for the F-35A

Next Generation Fighter Capability
Comparison of Costing

		Department of National Defence Program-based Analysis	Cost		Parliamentary Budget Officer Estimates
ACQUISITION	Production (1)	$6.0B CAD uses average unit cost of $75M USD per aircraft, acquired between 2016 and 2022 plus the following: + Accounts for predicted U.S. exchange rates + F-35A costs obtained from the **2009 Selected Acquisition Report** and reflects 2002 dollars adjusted for inflation in the years of delivery. + Includes potential modifications such as an Air-to-Air Refuelling Probe and a Drag Chute (development, material and installation) + Includes two block upgrades (Block 4 and Block 5) estimated at 2% of acquisition costs per upgrade **2009 Selected Acquisition Report** • Based on actual production costs • Annual validation by 9 partner nations • Economies of scale – takes into account high annual production rate • Reviewed by **Joint Estimating Team** • Validated by 120 experts - **2010 Technical Baseline Review** • Actual contract cost of aircraft tracking **below** all estimates Research & Development costs borne by US Acquisition at lowest cost in production during years of maximum annual production of aircraft	$6.0B CAD	$9.7B USD	Unit cost of F-35 A is estimated at $148M USD per aircraft acquired between 2016 and 2022 • Uses top down, parametric estimate • Primarily based on historical costs of fighter aircraft per **pound/kilogram** • Historical data not provided • Does not factor economies of scale due to high annual production rate • Assumes average unit cost of 2478 aircraft at $128.8M USD using their costing model. • Based on a learning curve model with only three data points including unsubstantiated average unit cost • No evidence of model validation • $1.5B error in the calculation of the learning curve which represents $200M in the calculation of the cost for sustainment
	Initial Logistics Set-up (2)	Estimates from the JSF Program Office analysis of the Department of National Defence *"Ground Rules and Assumptions"* for the sustainment of the Canadian F-35A fleet. Includes detailed estimates for: • Initial consumable and capital spares • Maintainer and Pilot Training Devices • Canada's contribution to stand up of Global Sustainment System	$1.3B CAD	$1.7B USD	Based on 18% of the Parliamentary Budget Officer's cost estimate for acquisition of $9.7B USD, where 18% appears to be derived from a 2001 academic paper on life cycle cost simulation using a simplified case study presented at a conference
	Project Management (3)	Resources required to further the project: • Staff salaries • Office space/equipment • Travel	$0.2B CAD	$0	Not addressed in PBO report
	Infrastructure (4)	Facility upgrades required at: • Main Operating Bases • Deployed Operating Bases • Forward Operating Locations	$0.4B CAD	$0	Not addressed in PBO report
	Weapons (5)	Requirement to provide an initial combat capability to include: • Air-to-Air weapons • Air-to-Surface weapons	$0.3B CAD	$0	Not addressed in PBO report
	Contingency (6)	Approximately 10% of overall project costs • To manage unforecasted changes to the rate of foreign currency exchange and the rate of inflation • To manage unforeseen circumstances or developments within the project	$0.8B CAD	$0	Not addressed in PBO report
		TOTAL DND ACQUISITION COSTS	**$9.0B CAD**	**$11.4B USD**	**TOTAL PBO ESTIMATES**

Next Generation Fighter Capability
Comparison of Costing

		Department of National Defence Program-based Analysis	Cost		Parliamentary Budget Officer Estimates
MAINTENANCE	Operating and Support (7)	Estimates derived from the Department of National Defence detailed *"Ground Rules and Assumptions"* for **20 years of in-service support** to include: • F-35 sustained as a global fleet of 3000+ aircraft with unprecedented economies of scale including shared non-recurring costs • Annual sustainment costs of $250-$300M per year which is equivalent to other modern fighter aircraft • 20 years for in-service support, logistic support, software reprogramming	$5.7B CAD	$14.0B USD	Based on an annual cost (**for 30 years**) of 6.4% of the Parliamentary Budget Officer's cost estimate for acquisition of $9.7B USD • The PBO states that *"Although the data that is publicly available is not sufficient to form the basis of a model as that used to forecast acquisition costs, to the extent that the data is available, the percentages returned by this model are believed to be reasonable."* However, the 6.4% is based on unspecified data and an unknown cost estimating relationship model.
	Overhaul and Upgrade (8)	F-35 approach to upgrades and follow-on development: • Software upgrade every two years and hardware upgrade every four years • Upgrades undertaken collectively and applied to global fleet with non-recurring engineering costs shared amongst F-35 operators achieving economies of scale when sourcing/contracting equipment	$0 **already included in acquisition costs at (1) and Operating & Support (7)	$3.9B USD	PBO using traditional approach to upgrades and follow-on development: • two major overhaul and upgrades (10 and 20 years following delivery) • Undertaken by nations individually, thus each nation pays 100% of non-recurring engineering costs and sources/contracts equipment individually Based on $30.4M (+/- $5M) per aircraft X 65 aircraft X 2 upgrades
	TOTAL PROGRAM COSTS - DND		**$14.7B**	**$29.3B**	**TOTAL ESTIMATES - PBO**

Next Generation Fighter Capability
Comparison of Costing

Next Generation Fighter Capability – Project Scope

The objective of the Next Generation Fighter Capability project is to acquire 65 next generation fighters to replace the CF-18 fleet on its retirement so as to maintain a manned fighter capability necessary for the defence of Canada and North America, and for Canadian Forces collective expeditionary operations.

This project will:
- *Acquire a replacement fighter aircraft for the aging CF18 Hornet.* The Department of National Defence will acquire 65 operational aircraft in accordance with the *Canada First* Defence Strategy, fulfilling a commitment to defend the sovereignty of Canadian airspace, remain a strong and reliable partner in the defence of North America through NORAD, and provide Canada with an effective and modern air capability for international operations;
- *Secure Logistics and Global Sustainment Support.* The Department of National Defence will secure sufficient spares and support equipment, and will participate in the Logistics and Global Sustainment Support concept;
- *Secure Training.* The project will provide initial on-aircraft training for aircrew and maintenance personnel in order to ensure a smooth transition to the new equipment;
- *Secure Documentation.* The project will secure access to all documentation, technical data and licenses required for operations and maintenance;
- *Support Infrastructure Requirements.* The project will support infrastructure enhancements directly attributable to the new fleet, such as upgrades to hangars, maintenance shops and supply stores. Most enhancements will be related to the security nature of the project;
- *Obtain Upgradeable Simulation Systems.* The project will acquire on-ground aircrew and maintenance training systems to support training requirements for the life of the aircraft; and
- *Acquire Weapons.* Where possible the project will use existing inventory to support assigned missions. To ensure that the Canadian Forces maintains a capability for high precision target standoff engagement with minimized collateral damage, the Canadian Forces will purchase additional weapons for the fleet, including advanced, network enabled precision weapons.

Definitions

2009 Selected Acquisition Report
All major US defense acquisition programs, including the Joint Strike Fighter Program, report annually to Congress via a Selected Acquisition Report. These reports include key cost, schedule and technical information. The Joint Strike Fighter Program Selected Acquisition Report information is summarized and provided to Joint Strike Fighter Program participant nations in a presentation format. The most recent Selected Acquisition Report information received by Canada is 2009 Selected Acquisition Report which is dated 24 March 2010.

2010 Technical Baseline Review
In support of a requirement for Nunn-McCurdy Certification, VAdm Venlet was appointed Joint Strike Fighter Program Executive Officer and directed to conduct a Technical Baseline Review of every detail of the program. The Technical Baseline Review involved 120 technical experts across the full spectrum of activities associated with a program of this size and nature (including manufacturing, aircraft production, flight test, etc.). The impacts of the Technical Baseline Review on the Joint Strike Fighter Program were announced to the public on 06 January 2011.

Joint Estimating Team
The Joint Estimating Team is a composite of the Secretary of Defense's cost analysis improvement group and estimating teams from each of the US Services. To date, there have been two (2) such cost reviews of the Joint Strike Fighter Program, JET I and JET II.

Ground Rules and Assumptions
In order to guide the cost analysis of the Next Generation Fighter Capability project, a set of Ground Rules and Assumptions has been prepared "FOR DISCUSSION AND COSTING PURPOSES ONLY". The Ground Rules and Assumptions are reviewed and updated regularly. In due course, the Next Generation Fighter Capability Ground Rules and Assumptions will guide the development of concepts of operations, sustainment, training, security, infrastructure, etc.

ANNEX 15

"New Stealth Fighters Lack Ability to Communicate from Canada's North"

New stealth fighters lack ability to communicate from Canada's north

Murray Brewster

Ottawa - The Canadian Press

Last updated Sunday, Oct. 23, 2011 3:42PM EDT

The Lockheed Martin Joint Strike Fighter is shown after it was unveiled in a ceremony in Fort Worth, Texas, in this July 7, 2006, file photo. The Harper government announced one of the biggest military equipment purchases in history on Friday July 16, 2010, to buy the F-35 Joint Strike Fighter from Lockheed Martin. (Ron T. Ennis/AP)

Canada's new multibillion-dollar stealth fighters are expected to arrive without the built-in capacity to communicate from the country's most northerly regions — a gap the air force is trying to close.

96 Annex 15

A series of briefings given to the country's top air force commander last year expressed concern that the F-35's radio and satellite communications gear may not be as capable as that of the current CF-18s, which recently went through an extensive modernization.

- Tories shrug off multiple warnings on fighter-jet price tag
- F-35 service costs may be more than double Ottawa's estimate
- Ottawa's fighter-jet estimate 'all hogwash,' U.S. watchdog warns

Military aircraft operating in the high Arctic rely almost exclusively on satellite communications, where a pilot's signal is beamed into space and bounced back down to a ground station.

The F-35 Lightning will eventually have the ability to communicate with satellites, but the software will not be available in the initial production run, said a senior Lockheed Martin official, who spoke on background.

It is expected to be added to the aircraft when production reaches its fourth phase in 2019, but that is not guaranteed because research is still underway.

"That hasn't all been nailed down yet," said the official. "As you can imagine there are a lot of science projects going on, exploring what is the best . . . capability, what satellites will be available."

Additionally, Canada's request to have the upgrade placed in the fourth phase will compete with software changes sought by other countries. Norway, for example, wants to use its own missiles on the F-35 rather than U.S.-made weapons.

Defending the Arctic is one of the Harper government's key justifications for buying the aircraft, which are estimated to cost between $16 and $30 billion, including long-term maintenance.

A Defence Department spokesman denied that the F-35's communications suite will be less effective than that of CF-18s, but acknowledged that so-called beyond-line-of-sight communications is a concern.

"Communications in the Arctic represents a specific challenge to all aircraft due to lack of satellite coverage in the north," said Evan Koronewski in an email response. "Canada is working closely with the other partner nations to ensure Canadian operational requirements for communications in the Arctic are met."

Air force planners recognized the problem last year and are "considering a back-up," said an April 2010 briefing.

A study is looking at whether an external communications pod can be installed on the F-35.

Mr. Koronewski said it is one of "many options" being investigated, but wasn't able to discuss other potential solutions.

The sophisticated pods, which are carried by the CF-18s, were purchased as part of the $2.6-billion fleet upgrade, which began in 2000.

The briefing to the chief of air staff noted that installing such pods could be made more affordable if other countries participated.

The communications problem is just one of several technical issues the air force is working on.

Annex 15   97

National Defence has asked the U.S. manufacturer whether it's possible to install a different air-to-air refuelling system on Canadian F-35s. Most other air forces in the world have stopped using what's known as a "probe and drogue" connection, opting instead for a plug-in receptacle which connects to a boom on the tanker aircraft.

The request was made because it's unclear when Canada will able to upgrade its air-to-air refuellers with the booms. Lockheed Martin says it can equip the F-35s to use both systems, but a decision on whether to spend money on modification has yet to be made.

ANNEX 16

"F-35 Production Costs Still Unacceptable, Pentagon Officials Say"

F-35 Production Costs Still Unacceptable, Pentagon Officials Say
By: Chris Pocock
March 18, 2011
Military Aircraft

Lockheed Martin is flying the first two low-rate initial production F-35s. Those airplanes will join the development aircraft in test flights this year.

The expected costs to produce and sustain the F-35 Lightning II Joint Strike Fighter in service are "simply unacceptable in this fiscal environment," according to senior Pentagon officials. Air Force acquisition executive David Van Buren and F-35 Joint Program Office chief Vice Admiral David Venlet told a U.S. Congressional committee hearing this week that their latest cost estimates are credible, after the various recent reviews.

The 31 aircraft recently contracted in low-rate initial production (LRIP) Lot 4 at fixed prices will each cost $111.6 million (F-35A), $109.4 million (F-35B) and $142.9 million (F-35C), they reported. These figures exclude the cost of the F135 engines, which are procured separately from Pratt & Whitney. The latest production prices for these are $15 million each for the F-35A/C versions, and $32 million each for the F-35B STOVL versions.

The Pentagon officials also revealed that the package of 19 F-35A aircraft offered to Israel for delivery beginning in 2015 will cost $2.75 billion.

Buren and Venlet said that after two restructurings over the past year, the F-35 program now had "realistic development and production goals, and a significant reduction in concurrency." However, they admitted that repairs to the stress cracks of the F-35B rear fuselage bulkhead that were discovered in fatigue testing will require that the 29 STOVL production aircraft already ordered be modified in three different ways, depending on their build state.

Meanwhile, Lockheed Martin officials have made optimistic statements regarding the stress cracks and other problems affecting the F-35B, such as the auxiliary engine air-inlet doors (strengthening needed); the engine driveshaft interface (to be redesigned); and unexpected temperatures at the roll-post actuators and lift-fan clutch.

As for other F-35 development risks rated as high, Van Buren and Venlet mentioned the "pilot vehicle interface" and the helmet-mounted display.

Lockheed has now flown the first two F-35A low-rate initial production aircraft at Fort Worth, Texas. These use the Block 1 software, which integrates sensors and communications, and have demonstrated stable performance to date, according to Van Buren and Venlet. The first six LRIP aircraft will join the 12 development aircraft in flight tests, under the restructuring. Another 10 LRIP aircraft are scheduled to fly this calendar year. But three development aircraft have still not been delivered: one F-35B and two F-35Cs.

Annexes – Source Information

Annex 1 – Extracts from 2006 PSFD MOU

Annex 1 consists of extracts from the 2006 Memorandum of Understanding (MOU) among Australia, Canada, Denmark, Italy, the Netherlands, Norway, Turkey, the UK and the US concerning the Production, Sustainment and Follow-on Development (PSFD) of the Joint Strike Fighter (JSF). JSF PSFD MOU was accessed at http://www.jsf.mil/downloads/documents/JSF_PSFD_MOU_-_07_Feb_07.pdf.

Annex A – Estimated JSF Air Vehicle Procurement Quantities as of 11 December 2006 appears on page 88 of the document cited above.

Annex A – Estimated JSF Air Vehicle Procurement Quantities as of 10 November 2009 appears on page 88 from the updated JSF PSFD MOU accessed at http://www.jsf.mil/downloads/documents/JSF_PSFD_MOU_-_Update_12_2009.PDF.

Annex 2 – Extracts from 2002 SDD MOU

Annex 2 extracts are from the 2002 Amendment Number 2 to the Memorandum of Understanding between the US and the JSF partners concerning the Cooperative Framework for System Development and Demonstration of the Joint Strike Fighter. JSF SDD Framework MOU was accessed at http://www.defense.gov/news/Feb2002/d20020207jsf.pdf.

Annex 3 – US Cost Definitions

Air Power Australia [website], 11 November 2009, accessed at http://www.ausairpower.net/APA-NOTAM-111109-1.html.

Annex 4 – UK and the JSF

David S. McDonough, "Canada and the F-35 Procurement: An Assessment" *Canadian International Council*, 29 October 2010, accessed at http://www.opencanada.org/foreign-exchange/canada-and-the-f-35-procurement-an-assessment/.

Rhys Jones and Mohammed Abbas, "UK Will Not Decide F-35 Numbers Before 2015" *Reuters*, 8 February 2012, accessed at http://www.aviationweek.com/aw/generic/story_channel.jsp?channel=defense&id=news/awx/2012/02/08/awx_02_08_2012_p0-422113.xml&headline=UK%20Will%20Not%20Decide%20F-35%20Numbers%20Before%202015.

Annex 5 – JSF Press Release, 16 July 2010

Government of Canada press release, 16 July 2010, archived and available at http://news.gc.ca/web/article-eng.do?crtr.sj1D=&mthd=advSrch&crtr.mnthndVl=8&nid=548039.

Annex 6 – Interview with Lt.-Gen. Andre Deschamps

Interview with Lt.-Gen. Andre Deschamps, Chief of the Air Staff, *Canadian Defence Review* 16:3, June 2010, p. 18. Accessed at http://www.canadiandefencereview.com/.

Annex 7 – AIT

Excerpts 506.11 and 506.12 are from the Agreement on Internal Trade (AIT) Consolidated Version, 2007, page 24, accessed at http://www.ic.gc.ca/eic/site/ait-aci.nsf/vwapj/AIT_agreement_2007-05_en.pdf/$FILE/AIT_agreement_2007-05_en.pdf. Article 1804: National Security is found on page 183 of the same document.

Annex 8 – Extracts from Treasury Board Contracting Policy

Extracts from the Treasury Board Contracting Policy are accessed from http://www.tbs-sct.gc.ca/pol/doc-eng.aspx?id=14494&section=text.

Annex 9 – Briefing Note – September 2006

Briefing note for the Minister of National Defence released under the *Access to Information Act* (ATI) September 2006.

Annex 10 – "UK, Canada Keep JSF Options Open"

Carlo Munoz, "UK, Canada Keep JSF Options Open" *Inside Defense*, 16 December, 2006, accessed at http://www.military.com/features/0,15240,120666,00.html.

Annex 11 – APA Stealth Analysis

Air Power Australia [website] 8 November 2009, accessed at http://ausairpower.net/APA-NOTAM-081109-1.html.

Annex 12 – "F-35 Defeated in Air Combat Simulation"

Eric L. Palmer, "F-35 Defeated in Air Combat Simulation," f-16.net, 7 September 2011, accessed at http://www.f-16.net/news_article4416.html.

Annex 13 – Boeing's Cost Estimates for the Super Hornet

Email correspondence between Alan S. Williams and Allan DeQuetteville concerning Boeing's cost estimates for the Super Hornet, 1–6 October 2011.

Annex 14 – PBO Cost Estimate for the F-35A

Parliamentary Budget Officer (PBO) Cost Estimate for the F-35A, accessed at http://www.forces.gc.ca/site/pri/2/pro-pro/ngfc-fs-ft/comparison-comparaison-eng.asp.

Annex 15 – "New Stealth Fighters Lack Ability to Communicate from Canada's North"

Murray Brewster, "New Stealth Fighters Lack Ability to Communicate from Canada's North" *Globe and Mail*, 23 October 2011, accessed at

http://m.theglobeandmail.com/news/national/new-stealth-fighters-lack...
ity-to-communicate-from-canadas-north/article2210678/?service=mobile.

Annex 16 – "F-35 Production Costs Still Unacceptable, Pentagon Officials Say"

Chris Pocock, "F-35 Production Costs Still Unacceptable, Pentagon Officials Say" *Aviation International News*, 18 March 2011, accessed at http://www.ainonline.com/?q=aviation-news/ain-defense-perspective/2011-03-18/f-35-production-costs-still-unacceptable-pentagon-officials-say.

About the Author

Alan S. Williams retired in 2005 after enjoying a 33-year career in the federal public service. His last 10 years were spent in the business of defence procurement, five years as ADM Supply Operations Service in PWGSC followed by five years as ADM Materiel at DND. In 2002 he signed the Memorandum of Understanding committing Canada to the second phase of the Joint Strike Fighter program. He is now President of The Williams Group, providing expertise in the areas of policy, programs and procurement. In addition, Mr. Williams is a Research Associate in the Defence Management Studies Program at the School of Policy Studies at Queen's University. In 2006, Mr. Williams authored *Reinventing Canadian Defence Procurement: A View from the Inside*. He can be reached at williamsgroup@rogers.com.